*When finished,
please return.
— Lucien*

THE TITLE OF THIS BOOK

Father Arrupe culled the words for his title of the present book from a statement of St. Ignatius which he has long cherished. It is found in the Saint's Constitutions of the Society of Jesus, [812]: "The Society was not instituted by human means; and neither is it through them that it can be preserved and developed, but through the omnipotent hand of Christ, God and our Lord. Therefore IN HIM ALONE must be placed THE HOPE that he will preserve and carry forward what he deigned to begin for his service and praise and for the aid of souls."

In Him Alone Is Our Hope

Texts on the Heart of Christ
Selected Letters and Addresses

PEDRO ARRUPE, S.J.

Foreword by Karl Rahner, S.J.
Introduction by Pedro Miguel Lamet, S.J.

Library of Congress Control Number: 2021941125
ISBN: 978-1-947617-14-8

Copyright 2021 by the Jesuit Conference, Inc., United States.

All rights reserved. No part of this publication may be reproduced, translated, stored in a retrieval system, or transmitted in any form or by any means, electronic, mechanical, photocopying, recording or otherwise, without prior written permission from the publisher.

Authorization to photocopy items for internal or personal use is granted by the Institute of Jesuit Sources provided that the appropriate fees are paid directly to:

> Institute of Jesuit Sources
> at the Institute for Advanced Jesuit Studies
> Boston College
> 140 Commonwealth Avenue
> Chestnuthill Hill, MA 02467, USA

Email: iajs@bc.edu
https://jesuitsources.bc.edu

INSTITUTE FOR ADVANCED JESUIT STUDIES
BOSTON COLLEGE

Fees are subject to change

In Him Alone Is Our Hope
Texts on the Heart of Christ
Pedro Arrupe, S.J.

TABLE OF CONTENTS   *page*

—*Foreword*   viii
—*The Sacred Heart of Jesus in the Spiritual Life of Father Arrupe*   xi
—*Abbreviations*   xxviii

Part One
Instructions to Jesuits

1. **Decree on the Sacred Heart:** 31st General Congregation (Rome: Nov. 17, 1966). 1

2. **What the Heart of Christ Means to the Society of Christ:** Homily at Shrine (Valladolid: May 8, 1970). 5

3. **Facing a New Situation: Difficulties and Solutions:** A Letter of Father Arrupe to the Whole Society Rome (April 27, 1972). 11

4. **The Spiritual Experience of La Storta and the Consecration of the Society to the Sacred Heart of Jesus:** Homily at Gesù Church, (Rome: June 9, 1972). 21

5. **New Formula of Consecration of the Society to the Sacred Heart of Jesus:** (Gesù Church, Rome: June 9, 1972). 29

6. **A Force for Transforming the World:** Reflections on the Apostleship of Prayer: Address at the Congress of the Apostleship of Prayer (Rome: May 4, 1978). 31

7. **The Mass in "My Cathedral":** Intimate unpublished notes (Rome: 1978). 43

8. **A Prayer to Jesus Christ Our Model:** Conclusion of the discourse on "Our Way of Proceeding" (Rome: Jan. 19, 1979). 57

PART TWO
Today's Theology on the Heart of Christ

9. **The Heart of Christ Center of The Christian Mystery And Key of The Universe:** Chapter of a book published in Australia (1981).   67

PART THREE
Pastoral Orientations

10. **Jesus Christ is All:** Interview given in Rome in 1981; published in Paris in 1982.   95

11. **Consecration of Japanese Families to the Sacred Heart:** Extracts from the book "I lived through the Atomic Bomb Memoirs" (published in Mexico).   99

12. **A Devotion for Our Times:** Homily preached at the Gesù (Rome: 1965).   111

13. **A Response of Faith and Love:** Homily preached in Rome (1973).   119

14. **A Feast of Sorrow or of Joy?** Homily preached in Rome (1975).   125

15. **What Can We Do to Present the Devotion to the Sacred Heart in the Climate of Today?** Some reflections of 1975 made public in 1983. Originally to an audience of clergy, religious, and laity (Rome: 1975).   133, 141

16. **Mystery of the Merciful Love:** Homily in Rome (1979).   141

17. **Father Arrupe's Spiritual Testament:** Conclusion of his address "Rooted and Grounded in Love" (Feb. 6, 1981).   147

— *Reflections in Retrospect: The Christ of Father Arrupe* - By Ignacio Iglesias S.J.   152

— *Father Arrupe's Farewell Homily at La Storta (Sept. 4, 1983).*   158

— *Another message to a provincial*   162

FOREWORD

There are certain undeniable experiences which, although rooted in the past, mark a watershed in the history of a person or institution; such experiences are irrevocable and they generate permanent norms for the subsequent existence of that person or institution. This is true of the Church, whose existence and identity until the end of time are guaranteed. Something similar, though with the relevant qualifications, is also true of a religious order. Normally, in the Church and in a religious order, only those experiences become the subject of explicit reflection which are associated with their origins, as for instance the experiences of the early Church, or the experiences within the founder's lifetime. Justifiably, these experiences are recognized as normative for all subsequent times.

But in the history of the Church or a religious order there are—'analogically' at least—experiences that, once they have taken place, assume and keep the value of a permanent norm. Without going into the history of the devotion to the Sacred Heart in the Society of Jesus, we can safely state that this Order did have, at a certain moment of its history, an experience that the Society has accepted fully: The devotion to the Sacred Heart though originating about 200 years after its foundation, it is something essential to the Society, which accepts it as a mandate from Christ, practices it as such and takes it as its duty to spread. The fact that this mandate has become more difficult, that this cult has to be revised theologically, and lived and preached in a way suited to modern times, all this does not deprive the Order of its conviction that this devotion is a trust truly received from God.

Here we touch something that may be difficult to understand from the point of view of theology and history of spirituality, but worth reflecting upon: That a religious order accepted and understood an experience as an integral part of its essence, so that it may not relegate that experience to the unimportance of the past, even though that experience did not occur in association with the origins of the Order.

This is the perspective within which we have to read the present texts of the 28th General of the Society of Jesus, Fr. Pedro Arrupe. These texts bear witness to his fidelity to the heavenly mandate accepted by the Order as essential to itself. They prove the passion for an identity maintained throughout history, even when the identity crisis knocks at the doors of religious orders as it does today; a passion for such a heritage as this devotion, which could be considered, albeit unjustly, as a phenomenon that could well be discarded as a useless relic of the past. Evidently this fidelity cannot work through reactionary conservatism. Handing down this legacy demands a creative fidelity that may revitalize it. This demands rethinking it theologically and pastorally.

Fr. Arrupe has taken up this task. The history of his life and his pastoral statements show how well prepared he is for it. The texts offered in this book show how he understands the *"aggiornamento"* of the devotion to the Sacred Heart. If we consider the enormous task of the Church, as the Church of this age and of the *world*, to proclaim the Gospel to *all* peoples and cultures, and if we further consider the dynamic transmission of this devotion to corning generations inside and outside the Society in the context of the Church's mission, then it is clear that the writings in this book do not exhaust that task. They represent one more step, a proof of fidelity to an unrenounceable experience of the Order, a sign of unbreakable and unwavering hope that the past can indeed give rise to a future full of promise.

The reader will see for himself Fr. Arrupe's contribution to this living re-interpretation of the devotion to the Sacred Heart. I only want to call his or her attention to three points so that his exposition may not be undervalued.

Fr. Arrupe appeals to the concept of *'Urwort'* (source word) to understand the word 'Heart' in all its depth. By so doing he orients the future theology of this devotion to the modern philosophy of language and to all that this modern science can contribute to a deeper knowledge of religious language.

Fr. Arrupe lays stress on the interior conditions to be achieved if we really want to appreciate the devotion to the Sacred Heart. Consequently he asks the theologians of this devotion to reflect on the subjective ('transcendental') conditions necessary to understand this devotion, that is: not to forget the *'fides qua'* and think too much of the *'fides quae',* thus applying to this branch of theology a tendency that is legitimate in contemporary theology in general.

Finally, Fr. Arrupe sets the devotion to the Sacred Heart in the general context of the theology of love and in this one love he sees the inseparability of the love of God and the love of the neighbor. This way this devotion can discover its deep relationship with the twofold mission that his Order has given itself under his leadership in the 32nd General Congregation, namely: The commitment to the Gospel for the ever greater glory of God *and* to justice in the world, without which man's *complete* salvation cannot be achieved. So, since the unity of God's and the neighbor's love is so much of the essence of the devotion to the Sacred Heart, this devotion has certainly a future ... in Fr. Arrupe's Order and in the Church.

Karl Rahner S.J.

The Sacred Heart of Jesus in the Spiritual Life of Father Arrupe

"What you are in love with, what seizes your imagination, will affect everything. It will decide what will get you out of bed in the morning, what you do with your evenings, how you spend your weekends, what you read, whom you know, what breaks your heart, and what amazes you with joy and gratitude. Fall in Love, stay in love, and it will decide everything." These words of Father Arrupe explain better than any speech could of the significance of the book the reader holds in their hands. In reality, the current pages become something of a collection of love letters, letters of a love that is unique but not exclusive, a love that is total and at the same time concrete, a love that is quotidian and defining, which led Pedro to give his entire life to Jesus Christ without reservations.

The heart is a symbol, something cliché if you wish, used even by children dedicating a drawing to their mother, or by anyone sending greetings to a loved one on Valentine's Day. However, it is always expressive and universal. Experts say that without a doubt, feelings reside in the brain, as do other faculties in human beings, but it does not occur to anybody to say, "I love you with all my brain." Perhaps it's because love can cause palpitations and feelings of warmth in our chest. It is there that we situate the center of our being.

The devotion to the heart of Christ is present in some form or another in the beginnings of Christianity, from the wound inflicted upon Christ by the centurion's lance at his death and in the devotions of many saints. However, we all recognize its flourishing as a result of the revelations granted to St. Margaret Mary Alacoque in 1675 as well as its connection with the Society of Jesus, thanks to the *munus suavissimum*, the special charge to the Jesuits to spread the devotion to the Sacred Heart that was recommended by the Popes and extended throughout the world.

After the Second Vatican Council there was a certain rejection of the devotion, mostly of the somewhat decadent forms in which it had been presented, such as the kitschy and somewhat effeminate images. In addition, there was resistance because of the sense that the devotion takes the part for the whole; or, as some said, centralizing Jesus Christ in only one "organ." However, important figures such as Teilhard de Chardin, Karl Rahner (see the prologue in this book) and Pedro Arrupe himself have, from the mystical perspective, expanded and contextualized this devotion, which is nothing other than putting the emphasis of the spiritual life on love.

This book gathers the principal texts of Father Arrupe related to this theme, but one will not comprehend them well without knowing his roots—the moments in his life which led him to that passionate love for Jesus Christ, from his childhood up to the time he became superior general of the Society of Jesus.

The Emotional Distress of a Child and The Devotion of a Novice

The first encounter with the Heart of Jesus dates to his early years. Pedro Arrupe, who had lost his mother in 1916, was a brilliant medical student in Madrid when he was called back, ten years later, to his birthplace in Bilbao. He tearfully saw a desolate scene: his sisters surrounding the bed of Don Marcelino, his father, who was gasping, struggling between life and death. For a moment Pedro looked out the window. As in previous years, Bilbao was preparing the procession of the Sacred Heart. And right in front of his house an altar was being erected, surrounded by a carpet of flowers. He then saw himself as a child with a candle in hand, following his gigantic father around the streets of Bilbao, as he did every year. Tears returned to his eyes.

"I looked out the window for a moment—Pedro would later write—and saw Father Basterra, S.J., approaching our front door. I rushed downstairs to meet him.

—How is Don Marcelino?—he asked me.

—Not well! He has already lost consciousness.

—Poor Perico! How the Lord tests us! But look, he said pointing to the statue of the Sacred Heart of Jesus, which at that moment was placed on the altar in the street—there is your true father, who died for you, but who lives forever by your side.

From this moment on, Jesus was my true father."

From his first step toward his Jesuit vocation, his knowledge of the poverty of the outlying districts of Madrid would be reinforced. During his novitiate in Loyola, he distinguished himself for his kindness, his prayer, and his austerity with himself. A frequent theme of Pedro's conversations with his friends was the devotion to the Heart of Jesus, something he would retain throughout the years without imposing it on others. At this time, during his years of formation, he completed the famous *El disco de Arrupe*. It consisted of a small booklet in which Arrupe had written some notes about the Heart of Jesus Christ and how to practice this devotion. *El disco de Arrupe* went from hand to hand in printed copies in booklet form. Before his death, Father Germán Arzuza (a companion of Arrupe) sent the author of this prologue a copy of *El disco de Arrupe*, which retains the rare aura of a relic. The pages of this small booklet, yellowed with age, were bound by flimsy, warped grey cardboard. It consists of four parts: I. Origin of the Question; II. Tremendous Importance of the Matter; III. Reasons for the Difficulties Encountered in the Practice of this Devotion; and IV. How to Attain and Sense its True Spirit. Its contents are a good summary of the books and discourse of the time about the Sacred Heart of Jesus. Arrupe would always retain this devotion, as we will see, although it will evolve with the passage of time in its mystical dimension as well as the way he presented it to others.

Following his philosophical studies in Belgium, on the eve of his priestly ordination, Jesús Iturrioz, a companion who had been a novice with him, recounts how that momentous occasion arrived for Pedro Arrupe. It was a time in which he was going deeper into the theological foundations of the devotion to the Sacred Heart of Jesus. He thought that this devotion was a strategy for the work of redemption: "I do not resign myself to the possibility that, when I die, the world will continue as if I had never lived"; and a few days later he adds, "We are so little, we can do so little and, the work of redemption is so great!"

In a handwritten note from that time, Arrupe wrote: "My ministries and my daily actions, my work, even that of today, will abound in fruit (not in the future but in the present), they exceed my hopes.... Lord, expand my heart with hope, as you widened yours to love us!" Days later, he delivered to Father Iturrioz a prayer to the

Heart of Christ, titled *Magister adest et vocat te* ("The Master is here and he is calling you": Jn. 11:28), which Arrupe had composed in August of that year. The text reveals clearly Arrupe's unconditional commitment to Christ. We provide the version amended by him seven years later in Japan, which he revised perhaps to improve on the pious style of the earlier years. This is the definitive formulation:

> *Jesus, my God, my Redeemer,*
> *my Friend, my intimate Friend,*
> *my heart, my beloved.*
> *Here I come, Lord, to tell you*
> *from the depths of my heart*
> *and with the greatest sincerity and affection*
> *of which I am capable,*
> *that nothing in the world that attracts me,*
> *except You alone, my Jesus.*
>
> *I do not want the things of the world.*
> *I do not want to console myself with creatures.*
> *I only want to empty myself of everything, even of myself,*
> *in order to love You alone.*
>
> *For You, Lord, is all my heart,*
> *with all of its affections, all of its loves,*
> *all of its delights...*
>
> *Oh Lord! I do not tire of repeating to You:*
> *I want nothing except your love and your trust.*
> *I promise you, I swear to you, Lord:*
> *to always be attentive to your inspirations,*
> *to live as you yourself lived.*
>
> *Speak to me frequently*
> *in the depths of my soul*
> *and demand much of me,*
> *for I swear to you by your Heart*
> *always to do what You wish,*
> *no matter how small or how costly it may be.*

How can I deny You anything
if the only consolation of my Heart
is in waiting for a word to fall from your lips
so that I may satisfy your desires?

Lord, behold my misery, my hardship,
my weakness...
Kill me before I deny you anything
that You might wish of me.
Lord, by your Mother! Lord, by your souls!
Grant me this grace...

On one of the copies of the prayer he adds a note to his friend: "Grant to him, Jesus, whom you love so much, that he may come to be a great saint and an apostle of your Sacred Heart. For me I ask nothing but: *Fiat mihi secundum verbum tuum [Be it done unto me according to your word].* For You: *Adveniat Regnum tuum fiat voluntas tua sicut in caelo et in terra [Your kingdom come, your will be done, on earth as it is in heaven].*

His Apostleship In Japan

When finally his dream to be sent to the mission in Japan was realized and he was able to throw himself more and more into his apostolic work, he had the opportunity to consecrate the chapel of some women religious to the Heart of Jesus, and it occurred to him to share this experience with Japanese families. He tells us how, at times, this prayer of authenticity and simplicity brought together in prayer persons of the same family who were of Buddhist and Shintoism belief, and at times it even produced conversions. Father Arrupe's simple behavior brought about a reaction of curiosity with the power to convince people. Those familiar with Japan and aware of the difficulties in obtaining conversions to Christianity there, could not help but be surprised at the early successes of Father Arrupe. For example, there was the Catholic family whose father was hostile to the Christian faith, but who still allowed his wife and children to practice it. The mother wanted Arrupe to consecrate their house in the name of the Sacred Heart of Jesus, but when he came to their house, the father was home. Arrupe was not intimidated. He went ahead with the ceremony. Suddenly a curtain opened, the father appeared, and he right away exclaimed: "I wish to be baptized."

What was the secret of this effectiveness? Father Arrupe would later recount in numerous homilies that it was his understanding of the Heart of Christ as the center of his person, his profound inner "I." In later years he would write: "In summary, here we have the simplest and most profound aspect of true devotion to the Sacred Heart." Contemplating that book "written inside and outside", we can learn of Christ, in whom are hidden "the treasures of wisdom and knowledge" (Col. 2:3). Contemplating and reading about the crucified one with the open wound of his side, we see in Him the Son of God "who humbled himself, becoming obedient to the point of death—even death on the cross" (Phil. 2:8). And going to Him, we will believe in that faith which, if it is true, will impel us to works—works of love of God, without doubt, but also of love that must manifest itself in love of others.

"If God's love is so great that He gave us His only begotten Son—'God has loved the world so much that He gives us His only Son' (Jn. 3:6)—our response to that love must be absolute surrender to Christ and to others: 'Become then imitators of God as beloved sons and daughters and walk in love, just as Christ has loved you and gave himself for us, offering Himself to God in adoring sacrifice" (Eph. 5:1). That is why Pius XII was able to write that in the worship of the Sacred Heart "is contained the sum of all religion and the most perfect life as well."

This way of life was already the most profound secret of the young Father Arrupe. When among his first Japanese contacts in the barracks of the Settlement, he could be seen going about with that restless and joyful spirit. He had the airs of a lover, a great lover of the "central I" of Christ. He seemed convinced from the beginning of his missionary work that the strength of his actions did not depend on him. Thus, wherever he went, he left a bit of his heart, and since he did not want to leave just his, he left a bit of the Heart of Jesus also. It was the secret of the universal spirit that would later break forth... That is why, after becoming Provincial, he consecrated the province of Japan to the Heart of Jesus on the 25th of July.

Regarding these experiences and his way of making Jesus present to families, young people, and children through devotion to the Sacred Heart, the reader will find some traces of his memories in this book.

Christocentricity, The Soul of His Generalate

Elected superior general of the Society of Jesus in 1965, Arrupe never forgot this special devotion. He withdrew to Villa Cavalleti, near Frascati, on July 24th to dedicate ten days to the Spiritual Exercises. His notebook of spiritual reflections reveals a generous heart in the style of Ignatius, a heart open to the "universal world," to the church, and to the Pope; it reveals an authentic missionary and a man of intense prayer united with God, not for himself but rather for the service of others, especially Jesuits. Thus, he unintentionally defined what his generalate would in reality become: "The superior general is the chief but also the head and the father. He is the ruler and administrator; but he governs with friendship, love, paternal simplicity, clarity, determination, and firmness..., with understanding, human kindness, tenderness, and love."

He felt that God was asking great abnegation of him, to convert himself into a "servant," "a little one" in the sense of the gospel, and this gave him "extraordinary strength." These dense reflections confirm the thesis that Father Arrupe, during the later years of his formation, had made "a vow of perfection" to God, a voluntary promise to seek His will and to fulfill it by choosing what was most conducive to this. "Now I must observe it with all diligence, since that diligent observance will also be my preparation for hearing and seeing and being an instrument of God." After his death a postcard was found in his room with the image of the Sacred Heart, printed in dark green; on the reverse of it was written the formula of his vow of perfection. It was his promise before God to choose the more spiritually perfect of any two options.

In various short, hastily written notes, his particular devotion to the Heart of Jesus and the Eucharist recurs: "The real presence of Christ, of my friend, of my great leader, but at the same time my intimate confidant. The work belongs to the two of us: He communicates His plans, His wishes; it is up to me to collaborate 'externally' with His plans, which He has to realize internally with His grace. What great work He places in my hands; this requires a complete union of hearts, absolute identification always with Him! And He will never turn away! I must demonstrate trust and fidelity. Never to separate myself from Him. But this love is rooted in *amicitia* (the love of friendship), in feeling in oneself the *alter ego* of Jesus Christ. With a profound humility, but with immense joy and happiness as well, I am always with Him! Always hanging on his words and wishes. What a happy life! Thank you, my God! Here I am, Lord!"

Taking advantage of the reference to God, a journalist asked him during an interview on the Italian television station RAI:

Many images have been attributed to this word "God" across the span of history. These images of God are especially for the use and consumption of the powerful to prevent the slaves from rising up in rebellion. But, who is this God for Father Arrupe?

The television producer chose a close-up; the red pilot light above the camera went on, and the camera zoomed in on the face of the superior general of the Society of Jesus. There was enthusiasm on Arrupe's face.

For me it is everything, no? For me it is everything; however, I would not know how to describe the face of God; I don't imagine him with a face, but there is something that completely fills my life and it appears in the features of Jesus Christ, in the hidden Jesus Christ, of course, in the Eucharist and then in my brothers, in humans, who are the image of God. So, I believe this sums up everything for me. Who is God for you? The answer is very simple: Everything.

Later, Arrupe would complete this response. Jesus was the prime mover of the life of Father Arrupe. "He has been my ideal since my entry into the Society, he has been and continues to be my way. He was and is always my strength. I don't think it is necessary to explain what this means: take Jesus Christ from my life and everything will fall apart, like a body from which the skeleton, the heart, and the head are removed."

Pedro Arrupe found the essence of this Christocentric interiority in the image of the Heart, which he learned in his novitiate and preserved intimately to the end. During his generalate, however, he spoke often of Jesus Christ and not so much of the Heart of Jesus. "There is a reason that we might consider pastoral," he explained, "especially with respect to the Society. In light of the emotional and allergic reactions which have manifested themselves for some years regarding the expression 'Sacred Heart,' a phenomenon that in part has its origin in certain exaggerations and emotional reactions, it seemed to me that it was necessary to let it go for a time, so that this emotional charge, understandable but in a certain way less rational, would disappear." Arrupe understood the "heart" as the "center," the "source" (*Urwort*), the primal word, and full of significance.

Thus, in 1972 he decided to modify the existing formula for consecrating the Society to the Heart of Jesus, which had been in force since the time of Father General Beckx (1872). With this in mind, he asked the Jesuit Fathers Schwendimann and Solano to write the new version. Thirty thousand copies of this text had already been printed when Arrupe, while making his Spiritual Exercises, called Father Luis Gonzalez one day after dinner and told him that Father Giuliani had offered to take him to La Storta. That was the chapel in the outskirts of Rome, where Ignatius Loyola, after asking Mary "to place him with her Son," saw clearly that "God the Father placed him with Christ," whereupon Jesus said: "I want you to serve us." While Arrupe was praying in that chapel, it occurred to him to write in that very place the new formula of consecration. The text, austere and profound, envisions the dedication of today's Jesuit as an extension of the grace and illumination received there by Ignatius.

Regarding his passionate love for Jesus Christ, we have already cited some examples of his notes on the Exercises, written just after he had been elected superior general. Here is another revealing text: "The personal love for Jesus Christ (for members of the Society) is absolutely necessary and is the basis for identification with him, that is, for being possessed by his grace in such a way that his thoughts are my thoughts and his desires are my desires... To achieve this identification is the ideal and the secret of true sanctification and of true fulfillment of my role as superior general, since I am but a rational instrument of His; not only a secondary subordinate (in the human sense), but a true instrument who should not act unless moved by the principal cause. What joy and happiness to be able to arrive at this!"

In his personal letters, Pedro Arrupe frequently refers to the Sacred Heart of Jesus. As testimony to the sensitivity with which Arrupe personally treated some instances of the tribulations experienced by veteran Jesuits, Facundo Jimenez, S.J. showed the author of this prologue a letter that impressed him greatly. It was dated November 30th, 1967: "Dear Father Jimenez: While somewhat relieved of work these past few weeks, I wish to express personally my appreciation for your sincere letter of this past October 5th. Like a son you open to me your heart, aggrieved by the deficiencies that you currently see in the Society. God must reward you for the life of prayer and sacrifice that you offer for the renewal of our Society. Continue doing this without ceasing to foster an unlimited confidence in the Heart of Jesus who is able to extract good from the evil that afflicts us and from our own failings and sins. Let us hope that those who are aggrieved by the current state of the Society may imitate you..."

Later, on December 3rd, a priest named Father Francis Peter Takezoe Tamotsu, who was wounded by the atomic bomb and converted to Christianity by Father Arrupe, wrote to him from Japan after he had fallen ill in Rome:

"My admired and beloved Father Arrupe:

I will never forget that historic day, thirty-eight years ago, when the atomic bomb was dropped on Hiroshima. I am currently reading with great interest the article that several months later you published in the *Catholic Digest*. I am completely aware of the need to continue to pray for true peace, which will make it possible to prevent such tragedy from ever happening again.

Today I received a letter from professor Kanzawa in which he tells of his meeting with you in Rome. I was deeply moved. How are you doing? I always pray for you, trusting in the providence of the love of the Sacred Heart of Jesus.

Thirty-eight years ago, on August 6th, the atomic bomb fell on Hiroshima.

Thirty-eight years ago, on August 9th, the atomic bomb fell on Nagasaki.

Thirty-eight years ago, on August 15th, Japan surrendered.

These successive tragedies led me to the edge of despair. It was in April 1946, upon returning to Hiroshima from Shanghai and not knowing what to do or where to go, that I had the good luck to meet Mr. Matsuda, a Catholic who took me to the novitiate of Nagatsuka on a Sunday and introduced me to you.

At that time, my despair changed into hope and my darkness into light; my heart was filled with courage, hope, and joy. My meeting with you signified my true encounter with the Lord Jesus.

From that time forward my heart has burned with love and supplication. When I think of you, I feel comforted by the love of the Sacred Heart of Jesus."

Perhaps the most complete synthesis of Father Arrupe's theological and existential thinking about the Sacred Heart of Jesus is found in his article, "The Heart of Christ, center of the Christian mystery and key to the universe," published in English in the United States on the occasion of the Centenary of the Missionaries of the Sacred Heart and included in this book. In this article he begins with his concept of the heart as the center, the *Urwort,* the primal word, which evokes more than it says. It is the interpretation of the history of salvation by Him who wished to be defined as "meek and mild of heart," since He lives in the heart of humankind and is the manifestation and bearer of the love of the Father: "He went about doing good." He preached love of enemy and of sinners, and he taught us to love "as I have loved you," since "God is love, and everyone who loves is born of God and knows God, because love is from God." In this text, Pedro Arrupe shows himself to be against the disassociation of love of God from love of neighbor.

On the topic of the cosmic significance of this love, Arrupe cites Teilhard de Chardin. In order to understand its importance, I must bring up a personal experience. When I visited him in Rome in order to collect information for my biography, he was already ill after a stroke, but I was impressed by his acceptance, his marginalization, and his loss of authority at that time, as well as by the great faith and trust with which he lived his bloodless martyrdom. At the time, since he could hardly read due to his illness, he held in his hands a large book of images about Teilhard de Chardin, the scientist, philosopher, and theologian who had not been able to see his work published during his lifetime and whom Arrupe had defended in his first press conference as superior general. Henri de Lubac, S.J. tells us in his book, "The Prayer of Father Teilhard de Chardin," that de Chardin always had an image of the Sacred Heart in his breviary. He had the custom of saying the Mass of the Sacred Heart the first Friday of the month and of reciting the litanies of the Sacred Heart, for which he felt the greatest admiration. "The Heart of Christ is something more than the Heart broken by our sins. The Heart of Christ is the center of all hearts, and of its fullness we have all received. It is the source of all sanctity, the fountain of all grace, the furnace of fire that sends its rays of love throughout the universe." For Teilhard, the furnace pouring out its flame was a powerful symbol for expressing an ontological reality that was mysterious yet no less real: the outpouring of the love of Christ which penetrates, transfigures, and consecrates the whole universe (P. Wenisch, S.J., *Teilhard De Chardin y la Devoción al Sagrado Corazón*, Dehoniana 1975/7, 1–12).

Father Arrupe states in the abovementioned article that Teilhard "made the most honest scientific investigation compatible with incredible tenderness and spiritual penetration. Teilhard professed a passionate attachment to the Heart of Christ." The Sacred Heart was the omega point of his universe. The world has a heart, and this is the Heart of Christ, towards which everything converges. Arrupe concludes that this love is trinitarian, and in a world characterized by unbelief, "God is discovered through the enormous emptiness that this ignorance and negation has left in our heart." He then adds what it means for community: "More than a community of faith—which it is—it is a community of love that is born from the community of faith."

Currently, after so much misunderstanding and suffering, the Church has finally begun Arrupe's process of canonization. Already around the entire world, hundreds of centers run by the Society of Jesus are named after him in explicit recognition of his status and his example for the present Society. He was a man ahead of his time in topics that today are recognized as indisputable priorities: inculturation, dialogue with unbelievers, promotion of justice as a consequence of faith, universal solidarity, the importance of migration, the grave problem of refugees, racism, the situation of the woman in the church, the savagery of capitalism, and a rigid system of thought. All these issues were already confronted by Arrupe in the twentieth century, always with the spirit of faith and optimism. "How can I not be an optimist if I believe in God?" So much was this the case that his last words before dying were, "For the present, Amen. For the future, Alleluia." The source of all this energy and the force that accompanied him all his life and during his nine years of Calvary resided in the human heart which he expanded until it fused mystically with the infinite fire of the Heart of Jesus.

Pedro Miguel Lamet, S.J.
Biographer of Father Arrupe

PART ONE

Instructions to Jesuits

ABBREVIATIONS

AAS—Acta Apostolicae Sedis

—Second Vatican Council documents —

AA—Apostolicam Actuositatem: Decree on the Church's Missionary Activity

GS—Gaudium et Spes: Pastoral Constitution on the Church in the Modern World

LG—Lumen Gentium: Dogmatic Constitution on the Church

—Jesuit Sources —

ARSI—*Acta Romana Societatis Iesu*

Const.—*The Constitutions of the Society of Jesus* (English translation by George E. Ganss, S.J.)

Sp.Ex—*Spiritual Exercises of St. Ignatius*

F.N—Fontes Narrativi de Sancto Ignatio

Form. Inst.—Formula of the Institute of the Society of Jesus (In the *Const.* translated by G.E. Ganss, pp. 63-73).

GC—General Congregation of the Society of Jesus

MHSI—*Monumenta Historica Societatis Iesu*

MI—*Monumenta Ignatiana:* The Writings of St. Ignatius of Loyola

I

DECREE ON THE HEART OF JESUS

31st General Congregation

Rome
November 17, 1966

Decree 15 of the 31st General Congregation on the Heart of Jesus was an answer to the numerous postulates received from the Society. Experts were consulted in the period between the two sessions. The Congregation members were particularly aware of the letter which Pope Paul VI had recently addressed to Father General and to the Generals of a few other religious institutes, urging them to foster this devotion in the Church. (ARSI XIV (1965) p. 584–587, 614).

Nonetheless, because the desires expressed in the postulates would have entailed a long and difficult theological investigation which exceeded the scope of the labors of the Congregation, the subcommission on the spiritual life judged that a formal decree ought not to be passed, but rather that it was to be recommended to Father General that he promote a theological and pastoral study of this devotion (31st GC, Historical Preface, 18, 3).

However, in the general discussion it was clear that this was not satisfactory to many of those present. Among those who felt strongly for the need of a special decree were the delegates from mission countries in Asia and Africa and those of Eastern Europe, who were convinced of the great significance of this devotion, precisely because of its symbolic values.

Father General himself, in the Congregation Hall (November 15, 1966) recommended a clear response to these requests and he personally with Fr. J. Onate prepared a draft which the latter submitted to the relevant commission. When the decree came to a vote on the very last meeting of the Congregation it was approved by a large majority vote (ARSI XIV (1966), p. 897). The electors had wished to offer the new General the opportunity to cast his vote on this decree after he had been absent from the hall the whole day, preparing his closing address.

This decree was expressly confirmed by the 32nd General Congregation in 1975 (d. 11, n. 43). In the promotion of this devotion, as pertaining to both the spiritual life of Ours and the apostolate, account should be taken—this Congregation says—of the differences which exist in various parts of the world.

Decree 15

DEVOTION TO THE SACRED HEART OF JESUS

1. The Second Vatican Council has shed a brilliant new light upon the mystery of the Church, but this mystery is perceptible only to eyes directed in faith to the eternal love of the Incarnate Word. For Christ, who "thought with a human mind, acted by human choice, and loved with a human heart,"[1] sacrificed Himself in human love that He might win as His bride the Church which was born from His side as He slept on the cross.

2. The Church finds a splendid symbol for this love, at once human and divine, in the wounded heart of Christ, for the blood and water which flowed from it aptly represent the inauguration and growth of the Church[2] and solicit our response of love. Devotion to the Sacred Heart, as proposed by the Church, pays tribute to "that love which God has shown

---

1 GS 22.
2 See LG 3.

us through Jesus, and is also the exercise of the love we have for God and for our fellow-men,"³ effecting that interpersonal exchange of love which is the essence of Christian and religious life. This is why devotion to the Sacred Heart is regarded as an excellent and tested form of that dedication "to Christ Jesus, king and center of all hearts, which our age urgently needs, as Vatican II has insisted."⁴ This should be the concern of the Society above all, both among its own members and in its apostolic ministry, not only because of our long and venerable tradition but also because of the very recent recommendation of the Roman Pontiff.

3. For these reasons the General Congregation readily embraces the wishes of the Supreme Pontiff; it recalls the decrees of earlier congregations concerning devotion to the heart of Christ⁵ and urges all members of the Society to "spread ever more widely a love for the Sacred Heart of Jesus and to show all men by word and example that the renewal of minds and morals, as well as the increased vitality and effectiveness of all religious institutes in the Church, which are called for by the Second Vatican Council, ought to draw their chief inspiration and vigor from this source."⁶ In this way we shall more effectively make the love of Christ, which finds its symbol in the devotion to the Sacred Heart of Jesus, the center of our own spiritual lives, proclaim with greater effect before all men the unfathomable riches of Christ, and foster the primacy of love in the Christian life.

4. It is no secret, however, that devotion to the Sacred Heart, at least in some places, is today less appealing to Jesuits and to the faithful in general. The reason for this is perhaps to be found in outmoded devotional practices. Therefore our theologians, men experienced in spirituality and pastoral theology, and promoters of the apostolate of the Sacred Heart of Jesus are urgently asked to search out ways of presenting this devotion that are better suited to various regions and persons. For, while preserving the essential nature of the devotion, it would seem imperative to set aside

---

3 Pius XII, *Haurittis Aquas*, AAS 48 (1956) 345.
4 Pnul VI, *Investigabiles Divitias*, AAS 57 (1965) 300.
5 Sec *CollDecr* 223,286 § I; GC 23, D. 46, n. I; GC 26, D. 21; GC 28, D. 20; GC 30, D. 32.
6 Paul VI, *Disserti Interpretes*, ARSI XIV (1965), 585.

unnecessary accretions and adapt it to contemporary needs, making it more intelligible to the men of our time and *more* attuned to their sensibilities.

5. The General Congregation also recommends that Father General encourage these studies. He will then be in a position to assist the whole Society to a better renewal of its religious and apostolic spirit.

2

WHAT THE HEART OF CHRIST MEANS TO THE SOCIETY

Homily at Valladolid

Spain
May 8, 1970

In 1970, Father Arrupe visited Spain for the first time after his election as General. At Valladolid he had a particular interest in celebrating the Eucharist with a group of Jesuits at the Shrine of the Great Promise (Santuario de la Gran Promesa), the church of the old Jesuit theologate of St. Ambrose. Where, according to tradition, Fathers Bernardo de Hoyos and Agustín de Cardaveraz received special confidences from the Heart of Jesus in 1733, and initiated this devotion in Spain.

This homily, as Father Arrupe mentioned some years later, expresses his most intimate convictions on the devotion to the Heart of Christ and on how the Society should bring the complete Christ of the Gospel to the People of God.

1. Importance of the Heart of Christ

We have been entrusted with the sweet task *("munus suavissimum")* of spreading the devotion to the Sacred Heart of Jesus, so fundamental in our spirituality which however at times, owing to some erroneous interpretations, falls into oblivion and disuse. I am therefore today extremely happy to have the opportunity in this Shrine to say that the Society of Jesus feels itself very closely bound to the Heart of Christ, because in this devotion it sees what the Supreme Pontiffs have ever so often told us: a compendium of all Christian teaching.

The Society of Jesus has undoubtedly but one ideal, that of serving the Church and serving the people of God, to bring Christ to the whole of mankind. And, as we know, the person of Christ comes to be known only when he is known in all the riches of his Heart, which on the one hand is the symbol of his love, and on the other has been the material organ that has beaten with the human love of Christ for men.

2. Knowledge of the Complete Christ

This knowledge of Christ is the basis of all knowledge. And Christ, who is the way, the truth and the life, has to be known under this meaningful image, which can be discovered in each page of the gospel when we read it at leisure.

This image is sublime, immense, infinite; it takes many shapes. There is the lovable Christ who is affectionate with little children; the Christ who denounces and castigates the hypocritical Pharisees; the Christ who commands the angry winds and tempestuous waves to be still; the Christ whose divine attributes seem to fade away and vanish in the dark hours of Gethsemane; the Christ who speaks with the greatest simplicity and utters at the same time the most sublime teachings, which no man can ever fully comprehend in their fathomless profundity.

And when we try to find the reason of this authenticity and unmatched uniqueness of Christ, we discover that there is an exceptional aspect in this figure—he is the Savior. Every page in the Gospel unravels the mysterious process of salvation through this exalted and divine person.

Christ is the Savior because he saved us, each one of us: "He loved me and he delivered himself for me" (Gal. 2:20). But if we search the gospels for the ultimate reason of the love that throbs in each of their pages, we shall find a further and much deeper reason. This love of Christ for men has a profounder Trinitarian source: The love of the Word for his Father.

It could be said that every line of the gospel, every word of it, is throbbing with the boundless love of Christ, who is burning with love for each human being and desires to ransom them in order to give glory to his eternal Father.

To the question whether this is the complete picture of Christ, the answer is in the negative; because Christ delivered himself for us, he laid down his life for us, but he rose from the dead. And Christ today is a living person. Where is he? He is at the right hand of the Father, interceding on our behalf; and in the tabernacle, the Eucharistic Christ. And searching for the reason of this intercession in heaven and of this real presence in the Blessed Sacrament, we find it to be no other than the infinite love of Christ for us, with whom he wishes to abide for all time.

Does therefore, this historical Christ, this risen and glorious Christ, this Eucharistic Christ, sum up the entire personality of Christ? Augustine gives us the answer, and this is No. "If you wish to love the whole Christ, you must open your heart wide; for Christ, as the Head, is in heaven at the right hand of the Father, but his presence extends to the whole world in his members, that is, in each human being."

Nor is that all. We know that the one and only person that is in Christ, that is, the Word of God, dwells in the innermost depths of our heart. This truth provokes St. Bernard's question: "Where is the one who speaks from the most hidden recesses of our souls? Which way did he enter? Did he enter through the eyes? Or was it through the ears or touch?" And the saint supplies the answer: "None of these ways, because this presence is something of my own intimate being." This, which is my innermost self, has been within me from the very first moment of my existence. It needed no door through which to enter. This divine Word, which dwells in the depths of my soul and speaks to me, is also the person of Christ. This is the complete Christ, the infinite love, symbolized in that Heart, which wishes to identify itself with us.

3. Bringing the Complete Christ to the People of God

Our only objective, therefore, as members of the Society of Jesus, is to bring this complete Christ to the people of God at this most interesting historical moment, a time marked by chaotic confusion and at the same time by a cultural evolution, out of which a new era seems to be emerging with the creation of a new technological humanism.

At present, we Jesuits, along with you all, my dear friends, are endeavoring to find ways and means to bring Christ to the people in an efficacious manner. This makes the present juncture a crucial one in history, beset with many difficulties, to which Christ alone can supply a suitable solution. *"Chommentsristus solutio omnium dijficultatum."*

Christ, the core of whose personality is love symbolized in this Heart, is the very same lovable Jesus Christ who walked this Earth two thousand years ago, powerful and at the same time helpless, who died on the cross for us; he is the same one present here in the tabernacle; the one again abiding in the innermost recesses of our souls, inspiring us what we ought to do. In Him we find the answer to all our problems.

All of us—priests, religious, and lay persons—all ought to feel this personal responsibility and not to take it lightly, because the philosophy of the death of God is more widespread than we might think. Let us not rest content with these ritual functions and religious practices, so consoling for us. Let us remember that outside the Church there are large numbers of the people of God who do not attend them out of unavoidable ignorance, or sheer impossibility, or perhaps downright negligence. We ought to be conscious that we are the heralds of Jesus Christ and should go out and contact this people who, in many cases perhaps with the best will in the world, find themselves, as I have said, outside the sheepfold of Jesus Christ. What is needed is the apostolic drive, the desire to work for Christ, the urge to bring Christ to the people and the people to Christ. With this, that total triumph of Christ our Leader will soon become a reality.

4. Trust in the Heart of Christ

For this task we count also with the promise of Christ who offers extraordinary graces. We need them today to combat atheism and to bring a spiritual outlook to a world more and more naturalistic. Christ is the only one that can give us the inspiration, from him alone can we get the strength to sustain our efforts and keep our hope alive.

This explains why the devotion to the Heart of Christ, founded on a theologically sound basis, is endowed with a profound solidity from day to day better known in the Church, and with a dynamic energy which can render our apostolate more efficacious and fruitful.

Today, when so many new sources of energy are being discovered, when we stand amazed at all the triumphs of scientific research in atomic physics and in the energy of the atom that may transform the whole universe, we do not sufficiently realize that all human power and natural energy is as nothing when compared with the superatomic energy of this love of Christ, who by giving his life vivifies the world. We, human beings that we are, can only transform already existing energy; but there exists an extraterrestrial source of energy which increases the energy of the world, an energy which has its source in the infinite love of Christ.

If we wish to transform this world of ours under its social and religious aspect, of the individual, the family and society, here we have the only energy that can achieve this transformation. This is the infinite love of Christ which we acknowledge with St. Paul: "He loved and delivered himself for me" (Gal. 2:20).

Thus, therefore, in this touching Eucharistic celebration in this Shrine we are going to come into close contact with this truly superatomic source of the Passion of Christ, who is going to offer himself on the altar. May an atom leap from this altar to the wide world, in order that everybody may know Christ's power.

We shall now offer this Victim, in union with this generous Heart that regards every human being with love. Let us also with generous hearts confidently ask him: "Lord, hasten the days of abundance, when the whole world will be your people. May this mystical Christ extend wider and wider, so that the day may soon dawn when we shall say that indeed you are the Head of the whole human race." With this intention we are going to offer this holy Sacrifice to the Father with the greatest possible devotion, asking these graces through Christ our Lord.

3

FACING A NEW SITUATION: DIFFICULTIES AND SOLUTIONS

A Letter of Father Arrupe to the Whole Society

Rome
April 27, 1972

This letter was addressed to the whole Society in 1972 which marked the first centenary of the Consecration of the Society to the Sacred Heart of Jesus by the General Father Peter Beckx. One year earlier, Father Pedro Arrupe had disclosed to the Provincials his intention of writing this letter and renewing the Act of Consecration. In this document that proves the intimate bond between this devotion with Ignatian spirituality and with the Society itself, Father General meets certain real problems concerning this devotion and outlines a theological position with regard to them.

During these hundred years, circumstances and conditions in the world and in the Society have changed a great deal, but challenges of change today require the same firm adherence to Christ and His Church that external pressures and persecution demanded of the Society then.

The letter was a response of Father Arrupe to the Apostolic Letter of Pope Paul VI on the Cult of the Sacred Heart to the superiors general of six religious institutes, whose special charism is the promotion of the devotion to the Sacred Heart of Jesus. This papal document "Diserti interpretes," dated May 25, 1965, was published in AAS XVII 1965, and was communicated to the whole Society of Jesus (ARSI XIV (1965) p. 584-587, 614).

> During the 31 years of Father Beckx' generalate, the Society witnessed a remarkable increase in numbers, which rose from 5,200 to 12,000. This was a period of favorable developments linked with severe trials, including expulsion of the Society from Spain, the banning of Jesuit activities by the 'Kulturkampf' in Germany, and the sacrifice of five Jesuit victims of the French Commune in Paris. The General himself had to transfer his residence from Rome to Fiesole, where it remained till 1895.
>
> In the eyes of the Jesuit General, the consecration of the Society to the Sacred Heart of Jesus was a testimony of fidelity to the mission entrusted to the Society by Our Lord of the promotion of devotion to His Heart, a source of encouragement and hope in the midst of the troubles of that time. The solemn renewal of the Consecration took place during a concelebrated Eucharist at the church of the Gesù in Rome on the Solemnity of the Sacred Heart of Jesus, June 9, 1972.

*

Dear Fathers and Brothers: Pax Christi,

As this year of 1972 marks the centenary of the Consecration of the Society to the Sacred Heart of Jesus by Fr. Peter Beckx, I would like to keep the promise I made in my letter of December 16, 1971 (ARSI XV, p. 766), and share with each and every one of you my thoughts on one aspect of the Christocentric spirituality of the Society: the devotion to the Heart of Christ.

Dear to my heart though this subject is, I find it difficult to treat of because of it the conflicting opinions found in the Society today regarding this devotion. I will therefore limit myself to expressing to you a desire I feel deeply as General; that of helping resolve the ascetic, pastoral and apostolic problems which the devotion to the Sacred Heart presents today.

Ignatian spirituality is, without a doubt, Christocentric. Like our apostolate, it is based on a deep knowledge and love of Jesus Christ the Redeemer, who loved His Eternal Father and mankind with a divine and human love, infinite and personal, with a love that reaches out to each and every man. It is this love of Christ, which a tradition of many centuries encouraged by the Magisterium represents in His Heart, which molds the Ignatian apostolate, making it a response on the part of those who "seek to distinguish themselves in every kind of service" and attain to the self—effacement of the Standard of the Cross, the *"kenosis"* of the *"vexillum crucis,"* and so cooperate in the redemption of the world.

1. Two Conflicting Attitudes

On this fundamental point it is easy to find general agreement. But when one attempts to treat of the devotion to the Sacred Heart, one encounters two conflicting positions which may be summarized thus:

Some maintain that the spirituality which they unabashedly insist on calling Devotion to, or Cult of the Sacred Heart, is something so distinctive of, so essential to the Society, that it should be the characteristic mark of every good Jesuit. For them, the Sacred Heart apostolate, that *"munus suavissimum,"* should be an essential feature of our pastoral activity, its inspiration and soul. The Sacred Heart, symbol of the divine and human love of Christ, is for them the most direct path to the knowledge and love of Jesus Christ.

Then there is a second position, that of those who feel a certain indifference, even some kind of subconscious aversion, to this type of devotion, and who will not speak of it. They hold that it consists merely of certain obsolete and anachronistic devotional practices. They find no inspiration in the symbol of the heart, because the word "heart" for many is charged with sentimentality; it excites distaste, even repugnance. The fact that in at least some cultures the heart is not considered a symbol of love except in a grossly sentimental context may contribute to this attitude.

These conflicting views have left not a few Jesuits greatly perplexed on the subject. They are convinced of the values essential to the Sacred Heart devotion, but they are at a loss as to how this devotion can be proposed in an acceptable manner to the faithful today. So they prefer to maintain a respectful silence and await further developments.

2. Reconciling the Two Positions

The first two attitudes may seem incompatible and mutually exclusive, but perhaps in their fundamental aspects they are not so. The first attitude is solidly based on the official documents of the Church and on the tradition of the Society: decrees of the General Congregations, letters of the Generals and other similar sources. The formation which they have received along these lines from the noviceship onwards, and their own personal spiritual and apostolic experiences have convinced them that they have drawn great profit from the practice of this devotion. Many of them point to the extraordinary fruits of their apostolic action, *"ultra quam speraverint"* as an authentic sign of its efficacy.

The opposite attitude derives from a series of reasons which vary from case to case. It should be clear that I am not referring to the more fundamental difficulties based on a Christological problematic which can go so far as to distort our very faith in Christ and the personal relationship we ought to have with Him. I refer rather to the various other motives on which some base their serious reservations in this regard. Some in fact experience a difficulty in accepting any type of spirituality that could limit personal freedom or give the impression of being imposed indiscriminately from without . Others hesitate to commit themselves to a spirituality that seems to them excessively individualistic and subjective. Yet others are turned away by the exaggerated importance given to private revelations, and by the claim that the devotion to the Sacred Heart, even the very concept of consecration, is based solely on them. It may be added that many experience an instinctive revulsion to the over—emotional, inartistic, and often tawdry representations of the devotion.

If these two ways of thinking are calmly considered they are not as conflicting as might seem at first sight. If one analyses the meaning of such reactions as, "Spare me your special devotions! Jesus Christ the redeemer, crucified and risen, is enough for me," it is immediately clear that they are intended as strong affirmations of a true love for Christ, who in the Paschal Mystery has achieved our salvation and calls us to identify ourselves with Him; and it is precisely this unconditional love for the person of Christ that has always constituted the essence of the Sacred Heart devotion.

When those holding the second position say they reject external practices as incompatible with the way people think today, those of the first group experience no difficulty in acknowledging that such things are incidental and of only relative and limited value. If the first group in turn insist that Christocentricity and personal love of Jesus Christ are absolutely necessary to attain one's true vocation in the Society, those maintaining the second position accept this fully, but caution against being led to exaggerate the "horizontal" relationship if one loses sight of the indispensable "vertical" aspect.

One could continue citing other points which in the light of sound discernment shed their intransigence and even tend to disappear. We ought indeed to foster such an exchange of ideas, provided they are characterized by the following characteristically Ignatian features:

—a broad understanding, which seeks to evaluate the statement itself and the spirit in which it is intended (Exer. 22);

—a complete objectivity, which knows how to consider the positive values and put aside one-sided exaggerations or purely emotional reactions (Exer. 181);

—utter respect for the legitimate freedom of others, without seeking to lead all by the same road, but allowing the Spirit to guide each one according to His will (Exer. 15).

3. The Objective Value of the Devotion

The objective value of the Sacred Heart devotion is taught clearly in many documents of the Church and the Society. It would be very difficult to maintain, and even more difficult to justify scientifically, the opinion that the fundamentals of this devotion are outdated or lack a theological basis, if one presents in its essentials the message which it offers and the response which it demands.

Christ, the God-man, by very virtue of being the incarnate Son of God, possesses all genuinely human values in their fullness. He is God, and at the same time the most human of men. He embodies in his person love in its fullest measure, because it expresses the

Father's gift to us of His Son incarnate, and because it is in itself the perfect synthesis of his love for the Father and of his love for all men.

It is this mystery of divinely human love, symbolized in the Heart of Christ, that the traditional Sacred Heart devotion has endeavored to express, and which it has sought to emphasize, in a world ever more eager for love, ever more in need of comprehension and justice. Between the Word of God and the pierced Heart of Jesus Christ on the cross lies the whole humanity of the Son of God, and the eclipse of sound theological understanding of that humanity has been one of the reasons which has led to the depreciation of the heart as symbol. To bypass the total humanity of Christ means to leave a theological vacuum between the symbol and the object symbolized, a vacuum which anthropomorphism and pietism are always ready to fill. To neglect the humanity of Christ means, above all, to lose the communitarian and consequently the ecclesial dimension of Christocentric spirituality.

The Church is born of the Incarnation. Rather, it is a continuing Incarnation; it is the mystical body of God made man. Hence there is nothing less individualistic than a genuine love of Christ: the very concept of reparation proceeds from an authentic communitarian demand, that of the Mystical Body.

Overcoming the psychological obstacles which the external forms of this devotion may present, the Jesuit should revitalize it with the solid and virile Christocentric spirituality of the Exercises which, integrally Christocentric and culminating in total commitment, prepare us to "feel" the love of the Heart of Christ giving unity to the whole Gospel. The life of the Jesuit is perfectly integrated in his response to the call of the Eternal King and in the "Take, o Lord, and receive" of the Contemplation for obtaining love, which is the crown of the Exercises. To live that response and that offering will be for each one of us and for the whole Society the true realization of the spirit of Ignatian consecration to the Heart of Christ.

From this intense living of the Spirit of the Exercises issues, with a certain inescapable apostolic urgency, the pledge to live and offer one's own prayer and work in union with the Heart of Christ and so attain to a life profoundly centered in Christ and the Church. The Apostleship of Prayer has long animated, and still continues to animate, the priestly perspective of many Christian lives, drawing them onwards to the Eucharistic sacrifice of Christ and the consecration of the world to God (LG 34). This instrument of the Apostleship of Prayer, which has so greatly helped the People of God in the past and with appropriate renovation and adaptation, render new and greater service today, when the need is so keenly felt to establish apostolic groups of prayer and earnest spiritual commitment.

4. Summary

It is a fact that the Providence of God has, at different times, provided the Church with the most appropriate spiritual means. For the Society of Jesus, one of those means has manifestly been the devotion to the Sacred Heart. None can deny the excellent fruits which have resulted from it for a Christocenric spirituality and the apostolate of the Society.

It is a theological certainty confirmed by the tradition of the Society, that the devotion to the Sacred Heart by its very nature possesses great values which can and should be applied to present day needs.

It is a fact that there are today many good Jesuits who experience no special attraction to this type of devotion; they may even be repelled by it. And an Ignatian principle tells us that we cannot impose on anyone a form of spirituality which does not help him in his life as a Jesuit (cf. *Fontes Narrativi* IV 855).

We find ourselves then in an historic moment of contestation; of criticism, even of rejection, of traditional attitudes. This entails great dangers, but it also has the advantage of compelling us to go to the very heart of things.

It follows that the Society, if it is to remain faithful to its tradition, has the duty of reflecting seriously on what is essential in the Sacred Heart devotion and of finding ways to channel and present it to the world of today. Simplistic solutions are unacceptable, both those which ignore the necessity of constant adaptation and theological development of its essence and exercise, and those which openly reject the devotion because it does not happen to possess an appeal for them.

A thorough investigation of this spiritual, pastoral and apostolic problem should lead us, on the one hand, to discover its true solution, which should be of great service not only to ourselves but also to the many, religious and lay, who in their perplexity are looking for concrete direction in this matter; and on the other hand it should help us to attain a deeper understanding of Him in whom are hidden all the treasures of wisdom and knowledge (Col. 2:3).

Profound meditation on the pierced heart of Jesus on the cross (Jn. 19:34) becomes a source of fruitful and very timely theological reflection. The Evangelist who expressly emphasizes the love of Christ in His passion and death (Jn. 13:1; 15, 13), seems to want to call our attention to this love as the keystone of His redemptive work by showing us the open side of Jesus, from which gushed forth blood and water, those mystical symbols of the gifts of the Spirit to the Church.

5. Conclusion

I would like as General, to add a personal word. I have felt an obligation to speak out on this subject so vital to our spirituality. Apart from the centenary celebration, apart from my own personal conviction of the intrinsic value of the Sacred Heart devotion and its extraordinary apostolic efficacy (to which both theology and experience testify), I also believe that it can be defined, with the Supreme Pontiffs, as "a compendium of the Christian religion," and with Paul VI as "an excellent form of true piety for our times."

I therefore wish to recommend to all, particularly our theologians and our specialists in spirituality and pastoral care, to study the most effective way of presenting this devotion today, so that we may reap in the future the plentiful harvests of the past. I am convinced that by insisting on this recommendation I am rendering great service to the Society, and that the more perfectly we comprehend the love of Christ the more easily shall we find the

3. New Situation: Difficulties and Solutions

authentic way to describe it and to express it. The graces promised *"ultra quam speraverint"* avail for us as well.

In the Church of the Gesù in Rome, where Fr. Beckx first consecrated the Society to the Sacred Heart of Jesus, I hope to renew that consecration on the 9th of June, the feast of the Sacred Heart, using the formula which I enclose with this letter. I would like all of you to join me in spirit in this consecration, in whatever manner each province finds most convenient.

May the Father, "who has hidden these things from the wise and the prudent and revealed them to the humble" (Mt. 11:25), grant to us, to you and to me, to know and experience more deeply day by day the inexhaustible riches hidden in the Heart of Christ. I consider this grace of the greatest importance at this moment in the history of the Church and of the Society. Ask, and it shall be given you.

Yours in the Lord,
Pedro Arrupe
General of the Society of Jesus

Rome, April 27, 1972
On the Feast of St. Peter Canisius

4

THE SPIRITUAL EXPERIENCE OF LA STORTA AND THE CONSECRATION OF THE SOCIETY TO THE SACRED HEART

Homily at the Concelebration Church of the Gesù, Rome

Rome
June 9, 1972

After the space of a hundred years since Father Peter Beckx, General from 1853 to 1884, had consecrated the Society of Jesus to the Sacred Heart of Jesus in the Church of the Gesù, Father Pedro Arrupe, who has always shown a very personal attachment to this devotion, renewed this act on the solemnity of the Sacred Heart in 1972, in the same Church which evokes so many undying memories to the Society and the city of Rome.

For the Prayer of the Faithful the intentions were read in a variety of languages by five Jesuits representing as many continents: there was a Novice, a Scholastic studying philosophy, another doing his theology course, a Priest, and a Brother.

Shortly before Communion, a special 'rite' introduced the act of consecration which Father General was going to read in the name of the Society. For Saint Ignatius and his companions, the pledge to "service" confirmed at La Storta took its actual form in the religious profession which the group made on 22 April 1541, in the Basilica of St. Paul-outside-the-Walls. Each pronounced his vows in the presence of the Sacred Host before

> *Communion, and this practice has always been kept in the rite of Final Vows for Jesuits. It was in like manner, before the Host and the Chalice, that Father General pronounced the consecration of the Society to the Sacred Heart.*

1. 100 years ago

As we are about to renew the Consecration of the Society to the Sacred Heart of Jesus, which took place in this very Church of the Gesù one hundred years ago, we cannot but instinctively recall the difficult days which the Society was going through when Father Peter Beckx performed that ceremony. These were his words in a letter to the Society: "If we look well into the world of men and events around us, fresh evils meet our gaze, and others arouse our fear for the future." And he added: "But in this perilous crisis of political affairs, I have been wonderfully cheered and consoled by the thought of the Sacred Heart that spoke those words, 'Come to me all you that labor, and I will refresh you.'"

As then, so now the situation of the world and of the Church is extremely delicate. We are today witnessing the birth of a new world, the appearance of a new type of man, the evolution of new patterns of religious life. Convinced as we are that the answer to these serious problems and the right adaptation of our life to the new circumstances is to be found in Him alone who is the solution of all the difficulties, we wish today to renew our Consecration of the Society to the Heart of Christ.

And seeking how we could best accommodate our consecration to the present time and the immediate future in accord with the Church's norms, I chose to consider the original spirit of our founder St. Ignatius by recalling his vision at La Storta.

2. The Vision of La Storta

Someone might think: What has La Storta to do with the devotion to the Sacred Heart? True enough; seen outwardly, there are hardly two episodes more different one from the other. At La Storta, a little chapel, solitary and abandoned, on the outskirts of Rome, a poor pilgrim stops to pray with two other companions. There the Most Holy Trinity communicates to Ignatius, in the inmost depths of his soul, a grace of the highest magnitude which will be like the synthesis of all his past mystic life and will become one of the most decisive graces in the foundation of the Society of Jesus. And here in the Gesù, Father General, representing thousands of Jesuits, makes this solemn consecration, whose echoes resound in all the houses of the Society throughout the world.

But if we examine these two events in their interior reality, we shall discover an intimate relation between the grace of La Storta and today's ceremony in the Gesù. There is no better key than the spiritual significance, the depth and the richness of the grace of La Storta, in order to interpret in an Ignatian way the meaning and the scope of our Consecration to the Heart of Christ.

Ignatius had for many years begged of Our Lady "that she should place him with her Son." This prayer attains now its fulfilment in the highest possible manner he could have imagined.

At La Storta the pilgrim feels in the depths of his soul that his vocation is that of being a companion of Jesus, and that the Blessed Trinity accepts him to be a servant of Jesus.

It is the Eternal Father himself who imprints in the soul of Ignatius this acceptance and promises his special protection when uttering those words, recorded by Laínez, *"Ego vobis Romae propitius ero,"* or the expression still stronger and more significant, which we read in Nadal and Canisius, *"Ego vobiscum ero."*

Turning then to Jesus Christ, who appears carrying the cross, the Eternal Father tells Jesus, pointing to Ignatius, "I desire you to take this man for servant;" to which Jesus, turning to Ignatius, replies, "It is my will that you serve Us."

This Trinitarian scene, so briefly told, reveals the granting of a mystical grace of the highest order, which therefore cannot be adequately expressed in human language. Ignatius is the first to acknowledge this. Hence the variety of versions of this extraordinary fact, otherwise fundamentally certain.

3. The Consecration: "Being Placed with the Son"

Analyzing, however, some details of the grace of La Storta we shall discover something of its rich content.

Ignatius' petition is heard by the Eternal Father himself. It is the Father who imprints in Ignatius the profound and unmistakable feeling of the divine protection. The *"ego vobiscum ero,"* "I shall be with you," is an echo of the biblical promises. This assurance was given by the God of Hosts to Gideon, "I will be with you ... and smite the Midianites" (Judg. 6:16). Thus did the God of Israel address the prophets: "Fear not, for I am with you" (Is. 41:10); "I am with you to deliver you" (Jer. I:8;19). This is how the angel put Mary at ease, "Hail, full of grace, the Lord is with you" (Lk. 1:28). Such was Christ's promise to his Apostles, "I am with you always, to the close of the age" (Mt. 28:20), and also to Paul at Corinth, "Do not be afraid, but speak, for I am with you" (Acts 18: 9).

Ignatius may now feel sure. If God is in his favor, who can prevail against him?

This is a key petition very dear to Ignatius, that "of being placed with the Son." This phrase, grammatically ungainly and somewhat harsh, expresses the aspiration to a more intimate proximity to Jesus Christ than he had before, to a more personal mutual interiority with Him. This is something similar to what St. Teresa of Avila called "spiritual espousals," and Mary of the Incarnation "gift of the Spirit of the Word Incarnate" (Letter of Feb. 2, 1649: *Ecrits spirituels* IV, 258–262). Ignatius prayed for this grace so ardently, because he foresaw how necessary and transcendental it was for the attainment of the apostolic ideal he had conceived in his mind.

The Eternal Father takes the initiative and exposes Ignatius' desire to Jesus Christ: "I desire that you take this man for servant." And in his turn Jesus Christ, who always does his Father's will, answers addressing Ignatius: "It is my will that you serve Us." He does not say "that you serve me" but "that you serve Us," taking Ignatius as his servant and of the Trinity.

Thus Ignatius' offering is accepted by the Word Incarnate. A most profound transformation is effected in the soul of Ignatius, more intimate than the one he experienced on the bank of the Cardoner. There he felt as though a new understanding had been given him; here he feels accepted and introduced, as it were, into the trinitarian life, in that intimate "circle" of the Trinity (MI, ser. III, vol. I, 132), whence he is sent *"ad extra"* with Christ to *serve him* in behalf of souls, a new service which he will later define in the Formula of the Institute as "serving the Church under the Roman Pontiff" and as "the defense and propagation of the faith."

The word "service," so typically Ignatian, takes on its full significance. It is this service that expresses the very goal of the Exercises and sums up the oblation of the Kingdom, of the Two Standards, and the Three Degrees of Humility. In future to serve will stand for a total consecration to the service of the Trinity, as a companion of Jesus in poverty and total denial of self, on the cross. Ignatius understands the deep meaning of his vocation and that of his companions, and feels himself not only called and admitted but also penetrated and interiorly transformed as the Apostles were (Lagrange, *L'Evangile selon St. Jean,* Paris 1936, pp. 447-448). So great was his interior force and courage that he felt capable even of dying on the cross: "I do not know what is in store for us," he repeated "perhaps we shall be crucified in Rome."

The grace of La Storta, a true compendium of the mystical experience of Ignatius, marks and illumines the spiritual trajectory of the Society. It also helps us to understand the meaning of our vocation: in every historical perspective, our life must be a ceaseless service of the Trinity with Christ poor.

4. Under the Standard of the Cross

Faced with the mandate of the *"munus suavissimum"* entrusted to the Society, of living and spreading the devotion to the Sacred Heart, what other meaning can be given to the consecration of the Society to the Sacred Heart, made a hundred years ago by Father Beckx and which we wish to renew today, than that of a total and unconditional commitment to the service of Christ and of the Trinity?

Francis Borgia, Canisius, La Colombiere and many other great Jesuits have understood the service under the standard of the cross along the lines taught by La Storta. To Ignatius, Jesus appeared carrying the cross on his shoulders; to us he presents himself today as nailed to the cross, with his side transfixed and his heart open; the heart, a symbol of love, from which flow blood and water, a mystical expression of the Church. The standard of the cross acquires here a new meaning; it reveals a more personal aspect, profound and dynamic. It preserves for us the abiding memory that at the root of the whole mystery of the Incarnation and Redemption there lies the infinite and human love of Christ.

This constant memory of what is most intimate in Christ's personality, his love to the Father and to us, is a fresh element added to the vision of La Storta, which helps to understand its meaning and to keep alive in our minds its importance and its relation to us.

It is hence clear that La Storta helps us to penetrate more profoundly into the true Ignatian meaning of our consecration and the rich content of the message of La Storta. It makes us know the person of Christ more intimately and steeps us more deeply in the import of our mission, thus making us more Ignatian and more authentic "companions of Jesus."

What is, therefore, the consecration we are going to make in a few moments? It is nothing else, as Leo XIII said in *"Annum sacrum,"* on the occasion of the consecration of the human race at the dawn of this century, than a surrender and commitment to Jesus Christ; for whatever is offered to the Sacred Heart of Jesus, as a gift of one's devotion, is actually given to the person of Jesus Christ" (ASS XXXI, 649, year 1899).

This surrender, this offering, the *"suscipe,"* is an act *of faith,* because it is a confession of the Blessed Trinity. It is an unconditional surrender to the Word Incarnate and to the Church his Mystical Body, translated into a special fidelity to the Vicar of Christ, which Ignatius called "principle and foundation of the Society." It is an act of *hope,* for we know that in order to accomplish what we promise we can count with the Lord's help: *"Ego vobiscum ero."* If God is for us, who is against us?" (Rom. 8:31). From experience we know the abundance of graces that have flown from fidelity to this devotion. Finally, this is an act of *love,* because we make a total offering as a holocaust, fully conscious of its implications; we know the meaning of "laying down one's life for one's friends" and of following Jesus Crucified to the end.

5. In the World of Today

The world stands in need of these men of faith, men stout Hearted and selfless, full of trust, ready to lay down their lives for others. Our mission in today's world is too arduous for us to accomplish it without special graces. Hence our prayer to Mary "that she place us with her Son," that she obtain for us from the Eternal Father, as she obtained for Ignatius, that special mutual intimacy which is absolutely necessary not only to withstand the world but to bring it to Christ. This grace of intimacy will effect in our soul that interior transformation which amounts to a "re-creation" of our faculties. It will be an identification with Christ that will achieve, in the words of Nadal, "that we understand with his intellect will with his will, remember with his memory, and that our being, our life and our activity be not in us but in Christ." (MHSI vol. 90, 122). This is an interior transformation that impels us to a greater love of the Trinity, of Christ, of the Church and of souls, and to reach the Ignatian level of true "companions of Jesus." This will bring about the change of our heart of stone into a heart of flesh (cf. Ez. 36:26), that will make us aware, as in the case of Ignatius, that God is always in us and with us, and that we may feel this, in an Ignatian phrase, "as a weight in our innermost soul."

This is the reason why our act of consecration ends with the words of the *"suscipe."* This *"suscipe,"* the synthesis and climax of the Exercises is meant to signify the personal element of our commit the concrete realization of a holocaust "in an odor of sweetness" (Const. 540). When this is accepted we have the guarantee that the necessary graces are granted to carry it into practice: "You will also bestow abundant grace to fulfill it."

Thus we see once more that the spirit of this consecration is identified with that of the Exercises and of the Constitutions. The most adequate testimony of our consecration will be that which will the better achieve the ideal of the true son of Ignatius and the authentic "companion of Jesus."

We conclude contemplating, with St. Francis Borgia, Christ our Lord on the cross: "in the wound of his side...taking it as a place of refuge and our oratory... and our permanent abode. Amen" *(Tratados Espirituales,* Barcelona 1964, p. 304).

5

NEW FORMULA OF CONSECRATION OF THE SOCIETY TO THE SACRED HEART

Composed and First Recited by Father Arrupe

Church of the Gesù, Rome
June 9, 1972

Father Arrupe desired to change the formula of consecration proposed by Father Beckx because it had been composed in a cultural context different from ours. He entrusted the composition of the new text to some theologians. In the end, he made use of the present official formula, which he himself had composed in the course of a day of prayer at the shrine of La Storta.

ACT OF CONSECRATION OF THE SOCIETY TO THE SACRED HEART OF JESUS
1972

Heavenly Father,

As Ignatius prayed in the small chapel of La Storta, you willed by a singular grace to grant the petition which he had been begging of you for a long time through the intercession of Our Lady to be placed with your Son. In your words to him you assured him of your support: "I shall be with you." You asked Jesus carrying his cross to take him as your servant, and this he did in turning to Ignatius with those unforgettable words: "It is my will that you serve us."

As the followers of the handful of men who were the first "companions of Jesus," we in our turn address to you the same prayer, asking to be placed with your Son and to serve "under the banner of the Cross" where Jesus is nailed out of obedience, with his side pierced and his heart opened as a sign of his love for you and for all men.

We renew today the consecration of the Society to the Heart of Jesus, we promise you all our fidelity and we ask for your grace to continue to serve your Son with the same spirit and the same intensity as Ignatius and his companions.

Through the intercession of the Virgin Mary who received the prayer of Ignatius, and before the Cross where Jesus Christ gives to us the treasures of his open Heart, through Him and in Him, we say from the very depths of our being: "Take, O Lord, and receive all my liberty, my memory, my understanding, and my entire will. Whatever I have or hold, you have given me; I restore it all to you and surrender it wholly to be governed by your will. Give me only your love and your grace, and I am rich enough and ask for nothing more."

On the Feast of the Sacred Heart
Church of the Gesù, Rome
June 9, 1972

6

A FORCE FOR TRANSFORMING THE WORLD

Reflections
on the Apostleship of Prayer
at the close
Congress of the Apostleship of Prayer

Rome
May 4, 1978

With these "Reflections" Father Arrupe closed on May 4, 1978, the International Congress of National Secretaries of the Apostleship of Prayer, held in the Curia, the first after the approval in 1968 of the new Statutes. These Statutes represented a rethinking of the Apostleship of Prayer according to the teaching and spirit of the Second Vatican Council. They aimed at inserting this Association into the general pastoral effort of the Church. They are concerned with giving life to an apostolic spirituality and developing apostolic prayer in priests, religious and lay people.

For Father Arrupe the novel presentation of the postconciliar Apostleship of Prayer was a creative force for the transformation of the world as envisaged in the Constitution "Gaudium et Spes" (2): "the world of men, the whole human family along with the sum of those realities in the midst of which that family lives, that world which is the theatre of man's history, and carries the marks of his energies, his tragedies and his triumphs, that world which the Christian sees as created and sustained by its Maker's love, fallen indeed into the bondage of sin, yet emancipated now by Christ."

This transformation is studied at three different but interconnected levels: that of the life of the individual

Christian, the social plane of the Church, and the aspect of Eucharistic transformation of the world. And Arrupe concludes with some practical suggestions regarding what the Apostleship of Prayer can do for the world today, and what the Society of Jesus ought to do, considering that the devotion to the Heart of Jesus, characteristic of the Apostleship of Prayer from its very beginnings, personalizes its transforming power.

*

Introduction

It is very important for us to understand the value possessed by the Apostleship of Prayer at the moment in which we are living, and to be aware of the new favorable circumstances in which it is placed and the effectiveness it can have in present circumstances; for today the world finds itself at a crossroads, not only that, but also at a time of creation of a new culture and a new mankind.

The history of mankind is the history of salvation; the philosophy of history comes to coincide with the theology of history. It is the spirit of God—he who renews the face of the earth—who directs the history of humanity. Man makes his plans, but it is God who guides the world: "A man's heart seeks out the way, but it is God who directs his steps" (Prov. 16:9).

We are able to discern this hidden action of the Spirit by looking at the signs of the times. The world, social phenomena, the course of human history are as it were a book written by two authors: the Spirit of God and human liberty, united in collaboration and forming a community which is a true mystery The mystery of Providence and infinite wisdom on the one hand, and the mystery of human freedom on the other. "We know that all of creation is groaning in birth pains" (Rom. 8:27).

The Apostleship of Prayer can and ought to be a great force for transforming the world.

When I speak of the "world," I do not mean it in a philosophical and general sense, but concretely and historically: as the generality of men and things that go to make up our present world. It is the world that the Council had in view

6. Transforming Force of the Ap. of Pr.

"The world of people, the entire human family seen in the context of everything that envelops it. It is the world as the theatre of human history, bearing the marks of its travail, its triumphs and its failures; the world which in the Christian vision has been created and is sustained by the love of its maker. It indeed fell into the slavery of sin but, through the Cross and Resurrection, Christ broke the stranglehold of the Evil One and liberated it *in order that it might be transformed* according to God's design and brought to its fulfilment" (GS 2).

The *transformation* here mentioned is effected through the world being assumed into Christ "so as to make a new creation beginning from this earth," which will attain to its fullness on the last day (cf. AA 5). The risen Christ is the beginning of this fresh creation: *Primatum habens.*

And this commencement is dynamically present in the Church—*primitiae creationis novae*—as a *transforming force*. This power works through the Word of the Gospel and the Sacraments, in the whole of the ecclesial Community, and it spreads to all creatures "who await the manifestation of the glory of the Son of God" (Rom. 8:19).

In the Church the *Apostleship of Prayer* is a privileged organ of this force. It "canalizes" it, and makes it present and operative. It helps Christians to live and work in that power. It is thus a choice means "for bringing to perfection" our and sisters in the Church (the purpose of the Society).

Let us now look more closely at how the Apostleship of Prayer is an instrument for transformation of the world: let us look at the facts and the potentialities.

I would like to distinguish three levels which are closely linked: (i) the individual Christian; (ii) the social dimension Church; (iii) the cosmic dimension: the world.

I. Transformation of the Christian's life

On the level of liberty, of the moral, free act. An essential for liberty is *intention*. Let us give the word "intention" its full force. Not intention as it sometimes is weakly understood, and conceived in an excessively exclusive voluntarist way, on the level of will; but rather let us consider it as belonging to the intellect above all, as in the great current of scholastic tradition. (Today we might more readily speak of "mentality," or of the "dimension" of conscience.) We could say that it is intention which gives *form* to the act. There can be several intentions in a single act. An intention may also be more or less "actual."

The Christian's great intention is identification with the intention of God the Creator, as the Council said in the text quoted above: "God himself wills to assume the whole world in Christ, so as to make a new creation of it" (AA 5), or as the Exercises put it in the Foundation; it is thus also identification—by the same token—with Christ's intention, as it is expressed in the "Kingdom" in the Exercises.

This intention was accepted by the Christian at the moment of baptism. But for Christian life to become more perfect there is need for this intention to transform ("inform") his mentality and be able to become an "actual" dimension of this conscience.

The Apostleship helps to actualize or realize this intention by placing it in "actuality": by bringing the great actual intentions of the Church before his mind.

This actualized and topical intention can transform man's life. By living in this new dimension the Christian will thus hear the appeal of God's will more intensely, and be readier to give a response.

Since this actualization of the intention is accomplished through conformity to the Church's great intentions, which are expressed by the Holy Father, the Christian will thus also live with the Church more intensely. So we come to the social aspect, the Holy Father's great actual concern at present, which ought to be integrated into the Apostleship of Prayer.

II. Transformation = Conformation with and in the Church

It might seem tautological to speak of the ecclesial character of the Apostleship of Prayer. Yet there are perhaps some community aspects in the life of the Church today to which the Apostleship of Prayer seems to remain, as I said, something of a stranger.

In the Church today there are many movements for community prayer: houses of prayer, prayer in base communities, in Communities of the Christian Life, rediscovery of common prayer in religious communities, and so many other forms. The Holy Spirit is at work in souls and in Christian groups.

We may here recall words which the Holy Father himself addressed to participants in a congress of prayer groups: "We rejoice with you at the renewal of spiritual life which is making itself known in the Church today under differing forms and in varying environments. Certain common features may be seen in this renewal...desire to give oneself totally to Christ, great readiness to respond to the calls of the Holy Spirit, more assiduous attention to Scripture, wide fraternal, commitment, and a will to make a contribution to the Church's services. In all this we may recognize the mysterious and discreet work of the Spirit, who is the soul of the Church... (*L'Osservatore Romano,* Oct. 11, 1973, p. 2).

We may also note that there are many Jesuits who take active part in these movements.

The Apostleship of Prayer is eminently ecclesial in its intensions, yet it has perhaps remained somewhat in the form in which it has so far been lived, rather limited to the individual

I would wish that the Apostleship of Prayer may enter more completely into the multiform movement of solidarity in which we are living in the Church today—without losing anything of its strength in the life of each Christian. The Apostleship of Prayer live and express such solidarity in prayer not only through common intentions and by means of written communications, but may it also creatively seek *new forms of prayer* in common, in religious communities, in parishes, and so on:

—Through practice of prayer of intercession in the local community. This prayer of intercession has perhaps been forgotten a little today, or at least it is not very much accepted, even though it is otherwise so natural and human.

—By entering into existing prayer groups, so as to make them more fruitful with the inspiration proper to the Apostleship of Prayer. Likewise with other active apostolic forces. (Perhaps these groups are sometimes a little closed, shut in on themselves. The importance of the Church's present intentions.)

—By accepting the Holy Father's watchword for the Holy Year: The reality of true reconciliation.

—By exploiting the possibilities which liturgical celebration gives us today for prayer of intercession.

—And so many other ways that the Spirit will suggest to you. He himself, who gives to each person and each period *"prout vult."*

III. Eucharistic Transformation of the World

The Apostleship of Prayer has always had a Eucharistic character. It might be said that the Council made its own that spiritual attitude which is lived in the Apostleship of Prayer, when it said:

"All their works (the laity's), prayers, and apostolic endeavors, their ordinary married and family life, their daily labor, their mental and physical relaxation, if carried out in the Spirit, and even in the hardships of life, if patiently borne—all of these become spiritual sacrifices acceptable to God through Jesus Christ (cf. Pet. 2: 5). *During the celebration of the Eucharist,* these sacrifices *are most lovingly offered* to the Father along with the Lord's body. Thus, as worshippers whose every deed is holy, the laity *consecrate the world itself to God"* (LG 34).

This "consecration of the world" is a *transformation* and a *sanctification.* The Council mentions this transformation and this sanctification when speaking of religious and laity:

" ... By their state in life, religious give splendid and striking testimony that the world cannot be transfigured and offered to God without the spirit of the Beatitudes. But the laity by their very vocation ... are called by God so that by exercising their proper function and being led by the spirit of the gospel they may work for the *sanctification of the world* from within, in the manner of leaven" (LG 31).

Men have been enabled by the paschal mystery to collaborate in the transformation of the human and natural world, which transformation is celebrated and mysteriously made present in the Eucharist, "the sacrament of the world":

"He makes all men free so that, putting aside love of self and bringing all earthly resources into the service of human life they may devote themselves to that future when humanity itself will become an offering acceptable to God.

The Lord left behind a pledge of this hope and strength for life's journey in that sacrament where *natural elements* refined by man are *changed* into His glorified body and blood, providing a meal of brotherly solidarity and a *foretaste* of the heavenly banquet" (GS 38).

There is the power and dynamism of the Apostleship of Prayer in the world of the future, as the organ and instrument of that Eucharistic and ecclesial spirituality which lives from this great intention of the Church's:

"Thus the Church prays and labors at the same time, in order that the *fullness of the whole world* may pass into the People of God, the Body of the Lord, the Temple of the Holy Spirit, and that in Christ, Head of all, all honor and glory may be rendered to the Creator and Father of the Universe" (LG 17).

PRACTICAL CONCLUSIONS

A. What the Apostleship of Prayer Could Do

How can the Apostleship of Prayer give practical aid to the modern world?

1. *By teaching to pray.* There is a real thirst for prayer, for contact with God, experience of God, dialogue with God. The "Teach us how to pray" of Luke 11:1 is of vital relevance today. To teach how to pray is one of the prime apostolates of our day; it means collaborating with the Spirit and laying the basis for every other spiritual activity, both interior and apostolic. Without prayer there can be no *Apostleship of Prayer;* this is why the first apostolate of the Apostleship is to *teach how to pray.* And to pray in the twofold dimension which is of the individual and of the community. These are two aspects, two forms of prayer which complement each other and stimulate each other.

2. *By showing the meaning and reality of the apostolate today.* To expose the reality of the world and its dramatic character, and show how urgent it is for the world to arrive at a solution, which cannot but come from God, from God who is at work and is moving men to act according to his Spirit. When understanding is gained of the urgency of the apostolate and the difficulties it has to face, and when we consider the apostolate in all its breadth, it is much easier for prayer to arise spontaneously.

3. *The Apostleship of Prayer as service to humanity.* One of the groups has mentioned this idea: Giving the Apostleship of Prayer the meaning of service to mankind; that is to say, to orientate the Apostleship's prayer and spirituality in the direction of impelling souls to service of their neighbors in the whole vast range of services that the Church lays before us today as being proper for Christians.

Not that we should go and transform the Apostleship of Prayer into a group of activists; but neither should we reduce ourselves to a group which prays but has no awareness of its responsibilities and the necessity to cooperate effectively in finding solutions for the problems of the world about us.

Today more than ever, the world is sensitive to those words of the Apostle James: "What benefit is it, my brethren, if a man say, I have faith, but has not works? ... Faith, if it has no works, is really dead" (James 2:14–17).

It is necessary to combine prayer with the service of action. This is a very Ignatian idea, and it is also dear to the present Pope, Paul VI (cf. *Octogesima adveniens*, n. 48–49). It ought to be carefully meditated and considered with a view to integrating the service which the Apostleship of Prayer already gives through prayer with other kinds of service, of a social, charitable order, etc.

4. Give instruction in a modern manner about the meaning of *"contemplativus in actione,"* "finding God in all things," *"contemplata aliis tradere."* These are expressions which concern a similar reality, even though there are shades of difference in the ways of considering the spiritual life. In the spiritual man everything ought to tend towards the unity of a life orientated *"ad majorem Dei gloriam."*

5. *Make much use of the liturgy.* Not only Holy Mass, which is always the center of the whole of the liturgy, but also the liturgies of the word or the paraliturgies, adapting them in such a way as to lead the world of today to pray for the apostolate and for evangelization.

6. Cultivate the domain which has so far been neglected *of prayer together with separated brethren,* and even with other religions, such as Islam and others that believe in the true God. This is an immense though sensitive field, and the Apostleship of Prayer can carry out valuable activity in it. It is certain that the Church's unity is the work of the Holy Spirit, and it is a mystery for the world of today how to gain that unity; yet it is no less certain that prayer for union and prayer *"uno ore et uno corde"* will be one of the most efficacious ways of arriving at complete union in the faith. Everything we can do in this regard will constitute excellent collaboration for that "union of Christians" which the Church and the Holy Father have so much at heart.

B. What the Society of Jesus Ought to Do

1. *Be convinced that the Apostleship of Prayer today retains its essential value,* even though it has to be adapted to the modern world in its exterior manifestations and applications.

We should even say that it is precisely in this age that it I greatest value, hence we should make a serious and effective effort to make use of it to the full.

For this reason it is for us (you and especially me) to try to present it to the Society in the most favorable way, demonstrating all its topicality.

2. *Pray for the Apostleship of Prayer.* In present conditions it will be very proper to pray to the Lord for the Apostleship of Prayer itself, so that he may enlighten us and help us to find solutions to the basic problems at present facing our organization.

And let us be assured that if ever the Sacred Heart ought not fail to accomplish his promise to bless us "beyond our hopes" and aid us, then it is very much the case today. It is for us to have much hope, *"dilatando spatia caritatis et spei. . . "*

3. Look for more collaborators. If the Apostleship of Prayer wishes to carry through a work as the efficacious result of its adaptation to the modern world, it needs more collaborators outside, but above all inside the Society.

The difficulty of finding young people who will enthusiastically and competently join in may be largely explained by the development going on in all sectors of the apostolate in the Church and in the Society of Jesus.

More concretely, in an apostolate like yours the difficulty is increased by the fact that numerous and varied problems are met with, of a theological, spiritual, psychological, pastoral order, etc. The Apostleship of Prayer is related to Christology, with the forms of spirituality, with the psychological significance of symbols, with ways of shaping pastoral action, and everything that that entails of diversity in devotions and exterior practices, which has marked the Apostleship of Prayer up to the present.

This is why I think that in order not to fall into a vicious circle—that is, not renewing ourselves because we have no young people, and having no young people because we are not renewing ourselves—we ought to try to provide the Apostleship of Prayer with an inflow of youth, and at the same time make sure that traditional methods shall be open enough for them to be capable of being renewed.

We have to avoid two extremes: to wish for young people to adapt to methods and a mentality they regard as old-fashioned, and to oblige present Directors to abstract from an experience and tradition and even a doctrine which retains many solid and essential features, even though some of its elements have been superseded.

In order to obtain real, spontaneous, and lasting collaboration from our own, it is necessary for us to be able to present this apostolate as something having great value today; this is not a result to be obtained from arguments imposed from outside, but from conviction arising from inner experience and reasons and necessary openness to well founded experimentation subjected to periodic revaluation.

Reference has been made on many occasions to lack of collaboration on the part of Superiors of the Society. I think our effort at persuasion ought to begin with some of them. When they establish the priorities for their Provinces in all sincerity and with a sense of their responsibilities, perhaps they consider the Apostleship of Prayer as something that was valuable once but has lost its relevance for our day. We will not gain anything by throwing our faults up in each other's faces; we ought to enter into constructive effort and engage in sincere dialogue so that all, superiors, those in charge of the Apostleship of Prayer, the young and not so young, may together rediscover those values that have to be rediscovered and give the Apostleship of Prayer a face and a reality which shall express all its topical value and convince everybody of its importance.

That is the initial work we have to do, if we wish to see the Apostleship of Prayer bloom again and be renewed in the circumstances of our time. So, set to work as soon as you get back to your Provinces. We will do our part here.

4. *Persevere in studying and adapting the way of presenting the devotion to the Heart of Jesus.* This will be another great service which the Apostleship of Prayer can do for the Christian world today.

There is need not only for theological investigation, such necessary for gaining ever deeper knowledge of the "riches of the wisdom of the knowledge of God" (Rom. 11:3), but also for pastoral examination of how doctrine is expounded and devotion practiced.

We cannot be blind to the difficulties which the latter presents today. It is a quite difficult point in catechetical pedagogy, and solving it calls for analysis of the various aspects of the problem: theological, psychological, affective, esthetical, etc. These ought to be considered in a practical and up to date way. Clearly this also calls for openness, comprehension, prudence, and patience; this supposes that we know how to put ourselves in others' mentalities, and understand them without condemning them a priori, even though it may be sometimes very difficult for us to allow certain positions, expressions, or manifestations.

CONCLUSION

The Devotion to the Heart of Jesus

We ought to thank God for the gift he made of this devotion to the Society. It is our treasure. This devotion is characteristic of the Apostleship of Prayer. It "personalizes" this transforming force, makes it something personal.

The glorious Christ—he who showed himself to Thomas the Apostle and let him see the wound inflicted by our sins, he who showed himself to St. Ignatius at La Storta, bearing the Cross upon which he redeemed us—is he who has shown us his Heart transfixed on the Cross, a furnace of love.

This loving attention to Christ glorified, wounded by love, *"agnus tamquam occisus,"* reveals the sacrificial nature of this life of prayer and action for transformation of the world to which members of the Apostleship of Prayer commit themselves.

Sacrifice means suffering, which means total forgetfulness of oneself, which means dying to oneself. Sacrifice does not only mean patiently bearing with the adversities of life. The Christian spirit of sacrifice is a supremely active attitude, it is a gift of oneself—*et omnia sua*—in love, with generosity having divine dimensions; it is a bond of love in which man cries out (in that strong, almost brutal prayer quoted by Father Teilhard de Chardin):

"Lord, enclose me in the depth of your Heart. And, when you have me there, burn me, purify me, set me afire, raise me up to perfect satisfaction of your pleasure, unto the most complete annihilation of myself."

7

THE MASS IN "MY CATHEDRAL"

Private Jottings Hitherto Unpublished

Rome: 1981

These intimate notes written in 1981 were put down without the author suspecting that anyone would one day read them. It was a literary outpouring of the spirit. The ailing General has now consented that these notes, however incomplete, be made public. In these effusions we get a glimpse of how spontaneously Father Arrupe has been living his intimacy with Jesus Christ in the celebration of the Eucharist from his little oratory in the heart of the Society.

This little private chapel of the General—his 'cathedral'—has been for Arrupe the power-house of incalculable energy and dynamism for the whole Society, a place of inspiration, a comfort and strength, even a living room of the most active leisure.

This was the place where for 17 years he performed the most important act of his daily routine—the celebration of the Eucharist. Here, identified with Christ, he felt himself to be at once priest and victim. As General of the Society of Jesus, he offered the prayer, works and sacrifices of 27,000 consecrated men scattered throughout the world.

As if talking to himself, in these jottings the writer pauses at the salient moments of the liturgy—the offertory, the preface, the consecration, the Our Father, the Communion and the final blessing—having all the time the body of the Society in his mind. United to the Heart of Christ—he writes—he felt himself to be a mediator between God and the Society and

> understood what St Ignatius laid down as the primary duty and function of the General, to be "closely united with God our Lord and intimate with Him in prayer and in all his actions, that from God, the fountain of all good, the General may so much the better obtain for the whole body of the Society a large share of His gifts and graces, and also a great power and efficacy for all the means which will be used for the help of souls."

1. My Cathedral

A mini-cathedral! Just 18 feet by 12. A little chapel which was prepared after the death of my predecessor, Father Janssens, for the new general...whoever this might be! Providence willed that this should be myself. I am grateful to the one who had the idea: he could not have interpreted the wish of this new general better. The planner of this tiny chapel may have desired to give the new general a quiet and convenient place to celebrate the Mass in greater privacy and where he might visit the Blessed Sacrament without leaving his rooms. Possibly he did not think that the little oratory would be the fountain of incalculable power and dynamism for the whole Society, a place of inspiration, consolation and strength... even a living room! It was going to be the room for relaxing in the most active leisure, where doing nothing everything is done! As the idle Mary drinking in the Master's words, much more active than her sister Martha! Where the Master's glance and mine cross each other. . .where one learns much in silence.

The general would have the Lord all the time, every day, next to him, with just a partition between them; the very Lord who was able to enter through the closed doors of the Cenacle, who made himself present among his disciples, the one who would be invisibly present in so many conversations and meetings in my office.

They call this little room the private chapel of the general. It is a teacher's chair *(catedra)* and a sanctuary: Thabor and Gethsemane, Bethlehem and Golgotha, Manresa and La Storta! Ever the same, ever different. If its walls could speak! Four walls that enclose an altar, a tabernacle, a crucifix, a Marian icon, a *zabuton* (a Japanese

7. The Mass in my Cathedral

cushion), a Japanese painting, one lamp. Nothing else is needed; that's all: a victim, a sacrificial altar, the standard of the Cross, a Mother, a burning flame that is slowly being consumed while giving light and warmth, and love expressed by two Japanese characters: God-Love.

Here is a program of life: a life being consumed in love, crucified with Jesus, in Mary's company being offered to God, as the Victim which is offered to the Father day after day on the altar.

In recent years I have often heard it said: "Why visits to the Blessed Sacrament, if God is everywhere?" My answer, some times unexpressed, is: "Really they don't know what they are saying; God is indeed everywhere, but 'come and see' (Jn. I:39) where the Lord dwells: this is his house. My appeal is not to arguments and discussion but to the experience lived in the house of the Lord: "One with much experience will speak with understanding" (Sid. 34:9).

"The Teacher is here and is calling for you" (Jn. 11:28). Here those requests rise spontaneously: "Lord, teach us to pray" (Lk. 11:1); "explain to us the parable" (Mt. 13:36). When we hear his words, we understand the expression of popular enthusiasm: "No man ever spoke like this man" (Jn. 7:46), or that of the Apostles: "Lord, to whom shall we go? You have the words of eternal life" (Jn. 6: 68). Then one understands by experience the significance of that sitting at the Lord's feet and listening to his teaching" (Lk. 10: 39; cf. Lk. 24: 32).

This cathedral is the theatre of the most important act of the entire daily routine: the Mass. Christ is the true and supreme priest, the Word made man. It is a divine attribute to be contained in the smallest place and not to be circumscribed by the Universe: this tabernacle or little tent is not too small for him, but the entire Universe is not big enough to hold him.

Each Mass has an infinite value but under some personal circumstances and in some special moments this quality of infinitude is felt more deeply. There is no doubt that the fact of being the general of the Society of Jesus with its 27,000 men consecrated to the Lord and totally dedicated to collaborate with Jesus Christ the

Savior, in all sorts of difficult apostolates, which may at times lead to sacrificing life in a bloody martyrdom, carries with it a weight of responsibility and a profound sense of universality of its own.

2. I Shall Go to the Altar of God

In union with Jesus Christ, I, a priest, carry with myself the entire body of the Society. The walls of this little chapel look as though they would crack. The tiny altar seems to become that heavenly "altar on high" (Eucharistic Prayer I) where the prayers of all the members of the Society ascend to the Father "by the hands of his holy angel." My altar resembles "the golden altar before the throne" (Rev. 8:3) referred to in the book of the Apocalypse.

If, on the one hand, I feel myself, as St. Ignatius would have it, "a sore and ulcer" (Sp. Ex. 58), "nothing but an obstacle" (*todo impedimenta*), on the other hand I find myself identified with Christ, "designated by God a high priest" (Heb. 5:10), "holy, blameless, unstained, separated from sinners, exalted above the heavens" (Heb. 7:26), "who has entered, not into a sanctuary made with hands, but into heaven itself, now to appear in the presence of God on our behalf" (Heb. 9:24).

With Christ I find myself too a "victim": "I saw standing before the throne...a Lamb as though it had been slain" (Rev. 5:6).

The Mass begins on this altar suspended, as it were, be tween heaven and earth. If I look *upward,* I can see the heavenly Jerusalem: "its radiance like a most rare jewel, like jasper, clear as crystal" (Rev. 21:11). But "I saw no temple in the city, for its temple is the Lord God, and the Lamb is its sanctuary" (Rev. 4: 22–23). If I look *downward,* I see "human beings on the face of the earth, in such great diversity in dress and in manner of acting. Some are white, some black; some at peace, some at war; some weeping, some laughing; some well, some sick; some coming into the world, and some dying..." (Sp. Ex. 106).

I am profoundly impressed at seeing from this altar, thus suspended between heaven and earth, all the members of the Society in the world, toiling and suffering in the midst of their endeavors to help souls, "sent throughout the whole world to spread his sacred doctrine among all men, no matter what their state or condition"

(Sp. Ex. 145). How I wish that from this altar blessings may fall as a mighty cascade, graces of light and strength that they need at every moment. In this Mass Christ will offer himself, and I with Him, on behalf of this world and this Society of Jesus.

Again, if I raise my eyes towards the heavenly Jerusalem, I see God's infinite holiness, "the Three Divine Persons, seated on the royal throne of the Divine Majesty, looking down upon the whole surface of the earth and beholding all nations in great blindness" (Sp. Ex. 106). Meanwhile the clamor of "We have sinned" surges all the time from the face of the earth, a clamor that resounds with the rumbling of a cataract: "the thunder of thy cataracts" (Ps. 42:7); "then I heard the noise...of many waters and the sound of mighty peals of thunder" (Rev. 19:6).

When I feel myself, like "the servant of Yahweh," bearing the sins of the Society, chiefly during my generalate, and my own countless personal sins, I appear "despised and rejected by men, a man of sorrows and acquainted with grief, and as one from whom men hide their faces. . . (Is. 53:3). Meanwhile I wish it might be said of me, as it was said of Jesus: "Upon him was the chastisement that made us whole" (Is. 53:5); "he was oppressed and he was afflicted, yet he opened not his mouth" (Is. 57:7). Thus while I hear the great penitential act of the Society, "We have sinned, and have acted perversely and wickedly" (1 Kings 8:47), I feel myself "the last of all, as one untimely born, unworthy of being called 'a son of the Society' (cf. 1 Cor. 15:8–9). This is precisely the feeling that permits me to sympathize with the fallen and the straying, and to grasp the whole meaning of those words of the letter to the Hebrews: "He can deal gently with the ignorant and wayward, since he himself is beset with weakness, he is bound to offer sacrifice for his own sins as well as for those of the people" (Heb. 5:2–3).

Christ becomes "the mediator of the new covenant" (Heb. 9:15). I too, in union with the heart of Christ and in spite of everything, I feel myself to be a mediator, and understand why St. Ignatius designates as the primary function of the general of the Society, "that he should be closely united with God our Lord and intimate with Him, that from the Lord, the fountain of all good, the general may so much the better obtain for the whole body of the Society a large share of His gifts and graces, and also a great power and efficacy for all the means which will be used for the help of souls" (Const. 723).

My position between God and the Society of Jesus, as a priest and during the celebration of the Eucharist, is that of a "mediator between God and men," to govern the whole body of the Society... This he will do primarily by his prayer which is full of desires and by his sacrifices, to obtain the grace of preservation and development... and on his own part he should hold these means in high esteem and have great confidence in our Lord, since these are the most efficacious means of gaining grace from His Divine Majesty, the source of what is longed for" (Const. 789–790).

The office of general thus considered appears in all its depth and in clear light: "morning by morning he wakens my ear...the Lord God has opened my ear" (Isa. 50: 4–5). Aware of my being a priest with the servant of Yahweh, "I do not wish to be rebellious or turn backward; I offer my back to the smiters, and my cheeks to those who pull out my beard. I hid not my face from shame and spitting" (cf. Isa. 50: 5–6). But how consoling it is to read in the sacred text: "When he makes himself an offering for sin, he shall see his offspring, he shall prolong his days; the will of the Lord shall prosper in his hand; he shall see the fruit of the travail of his soul and be satisfied; by his knowledge shall the righteous one, my servant, make many to be accounted righteous and he shall bear their iniquities" (Isa. 53:10–11).

3. The Offertory

I experience the profound feeling of standing before the God of mystery *(arcano)*, the *Agios athanatos* (Holy Immortal) and the *Deus absconditus* (the hidden God). I feel that he is present in me and loves me as a father, that he is the fountainhead of all life, and that he accepts my offering.

As I raise the paten, I try to penetrate with the eyes of Christ and with the light of faith, through the infinitude of the universe, to the very heart of the Trinity: "Blessed are you, God of all creation; through your goodness we have this bread to offer..." At the same time those words from the old text come to my mind: "which I, thy unworthy servant offer to thee, the living and true God." All my unworthiness faces me again: "despised and rejected by men, a man of sorrows and acquainted with grief" (Is. 53:3); "and he shall bear their iniquities" (Is. 53:11).

You know everything, Lord! As I raise the paten, it seems to me that all my brothers gaze at it, feeling themselves to be present: "and for all those around me." The paten seems to expand as "my innumerable sins and negligences" and those of others are accumulating, along with the aspirations and desires of the whole Society. Like Moses, I feel that "I am not able to carry all this people alone; the burden is too heavy for me" (Num. 11:14). I feel as though the hands of all the Jesuits of the world would help me to sustain this most heavy paten, loaded with sins but also with desires, hopes and petitions. I seem to hear the Lord say to me, as he said to Moses: "I will take some of the spirit which is upon you and put it upon them; and they shall bear the burden of the people with you, that you may not bear it yourself alone." (Num. 11:17). And then, as though the paten would become lighter or my arms stronger, I am able to lift the paten higher as if to place it nearer to the Lord.

"And also for all the faithful Christians, living and dead... and for the salvation of the whole world." I almost feel like fainting when faced with human malice and sin. I need that you stretch out your almighty hand, Lord. "I stretched out the heavens alone, I spread out the earth. Who was with me?" (Is. 44:24). Sustained by this powerful hand, I shall be able to carry on: "This bread will become for us the bread of life."

I now take the chalice with the wine which will be changed into the blood of Jesus. "Blessed are you, Lord, God of all creation. Through your goodness we have this wine to offer ... it will become our spiritual drink." This wine, fruit of the vine pressed down in the wine-press and fermented, will be converted into the blood shed on the cross.

This chalice, symbol of that cup that caused you to shed blood at Gethsemane, and that was so bitter that you wished you would not have to drink it, will soon become the chalice of your blood poured out for the salvation of the world. Into it are now poured the sufferings of so many Jesuits who, crushed in their turn, have given or shall give their lives for you in a bloody or unbloody manner, their tears, their sweat... a fowl unsavory mixture which, when united with your blood, will become pleasant and sweet-scented—the aroma of Christ (2 Cor. 2:15).

"We know that this is to be our lot ... to suffer affliction" (I Thes. 3:3), but irresistibly impelled by your charity ("for the love of God overwhelms us" 2 Cor. 5:14), we choose and beg "to be received under your standard... and bear insults and wrongs, thereby to imitate you better" (Sp. Ex. 147).

Certainly, you have heard our prayer, for the cup is overflowing, but charity makes us to be "overjoyed with all our affliction" (2 Cor. 7:4). This chalice, converted for us into united in the daily community holocaust, constitute a total sacrifice, *our sacrifice* of praise (Eucharistic Prayer IV).

Thus, bowing before the throne of the Trinity, I can say with the whole Church: "In the spirit of humility and with a contrite heart, let us be received by Thee, O Lord; and grant that the sacrifice we offer in thy sight this day may be pleasing to Thee, O Lord God."

Our Sacrifice: of Christ, mine, and of the whole Society, as a body united in the charity of the Holy Spirit, members and head with Christ (cf. Const. 6 1). United also with "the bond of obedience" (Const. 659), by which we all, as one man, offer the daily holocaust of our lives, "in which the entire man, without any reservation, offers himself in the fire charity to his Creator and Lord" (Letter on Obedience, March 26, 1553: MI Epp IV, 669–681). Our personal sacrifices, united in the daily community praise (Eucharistic Prayer IV).

4. Preface and Consecration

From the heart itself of the Society spontaneously rises that acknowledgement, "Father, it is truly meet and just, it is our duty and our salvation always and everywhere to give you thanks." Our song of praise would join that of the angels and blend with it in to a harmonious choir, every member of which sings in his own voice in a multitude and diversity of tones, similar to that impressive chorus formed by that "great multitude which no man could number from all the tribes and peoples and tongues ... crying

7. The Mass in my Cathedral

out with a loud voice, Salvation belongs to our God who sits upon the throne, and to the Lamb" (Rev. 7:9–10). Our song would join also that of the Society triumphant in heaven and that of all the angels and saints, "Amen! Blessing and glory and wisdom and thanksgiving and honor and might be to our God for ever and ever! Amen" (Rev. 7:12).

Following on this mighty chorus, I seem to hear a striking silence. "Be silent before the Lord God! For the day of the Lord is at hand; the Lord has prepared a sacrifice and consecrated his guests" (Zeph. l: 7). "Be silent, all flesh, before the Lord!" (Zech. 2:13). "There was silence in heaven for about half an hour" (Rev. 8:1). Let us, therefore, keep in the silence of our heart, as Mary did (Lk. 2:51), everything that is going to take place on "this altar in heaven" (Eucharistic Prayer IV), the mystery of the Passover, in which "Christ was immolated," the mystery of the Redemption of the world, the mystery of the highest glorification of the Father. "And they were filled with wonder and astonished at what had taken place" (Acts 3:10).

The sublime moment of the Consecration is drawing near. In union with the whole body of the Society, identified with Christ, I hold the host in my hands and pronounce the words, "This is my body": my body, that of Christ; "This is the cup of my blood": a solemn moment which can be commented only in awesome silence. Christ converts the bread into his body and the wine into his blood, but the one pronouncing the sacramental words is I! This identification with him is such that I can say, this is my body, but it is Christ's body. My inner self is all ablaze, as if I felt the Heart of Christ beating instead of mine, or within mine! As though his blood was coursing through my veins at the moment of consecration!

The mystical sacramental separation of the body and blood of Christ is a reality and a symbol, but he who receives the body receives the whole Christ and he who receives the blood receives the whole as well.

The redemption of the world was thus accomplished: incarnation, death, paschal mystery, salvation. All this is repeated at this moment in my hands. I remain "filled with astonishment," yet "I believe Lord, help my unbelief" (Mk. 9:24). Christ in my hands! The Lamb that takes away the sins of the world is not on the highest throne of the Apocalypse, but in my hands, as bread under the sacramental species... I believe! At the moment of the consecration the perfect glorification of the Father takes place; this will soon be expressed in the doxology: "Through Christ, with Him, and in Him, in the unity of the Holy Spirit, all glory and honor is yours, Almighty Father, for ever and ever."

At this solemn moment I pause a while, "in order to reflect and ponder, upon what presents itself to my mind" (Sp. Ex. 53). How does the world appear from this altar? How does Jesus Christ see it? In order to understand this I must enlarge my heart to world proportions. Like the Heart of Christ, the heart of the body of the whole Society must be enlarged, and with it the heart of each one of us. Ours must be a heart that embraces all men without exception, as the Heart of Christ "who desires all men to be saved and to come to the knowledge of the truth" (1 Tim. 2: 4), so that finally "there shall be one flock, one shepherd" (Jn. 10: 16).

From this altar, between heaven and earth, one gets a better vision and understanding of the needs of men in the vast world; one sees and understands, in a new light, the import of that universal mission: "Go into all the world and preach the gospel to the whole of creation" (Mk. 16:15). I personally feel myself, as it were, hurled to the world, and with me the whole Society sent to the wide world. This is its target, its allotted task until it returns again to glorify the Lord once the battle for the Kingdom is won.

My ears keep on ringing with those reassuring statements: "I send you" (Jn. 20:21), and "I am with you always" (Mt. 28:20). These words fill our hearts with confidence. My incomparable companion is Christ himself, who is not only present on this altar but within me, filling me with his divinity, and who sends me to those who did not receive him (cf. Jn. 1:11). My response can only be, "Lord, what would you have me to do?" (Acts 9:6), and "What ought I to do for Christ?" (Sp. Ex. 53).

The body of the Society, in its full awareness of being sent and strengthened with the power of God, feels rejuvenated and full of vigor and zest; it feels the blood of Christ coursing in its veins, and the fullness of the Spirit of Christ possessing its very being, as if propelled by the rush of a mighty wind (cf. Acts 2:2). Who will be able to withstand this Society if it faithfully follows the line of mission pointed out to it by the Lord? The Society knows that the life of its members is that of "men crucified to the world and to whom the world is crucified" (cf. Gal. 6:14), and that no one will be able to withstand "the wisdom and the Spirit which speaks" in such men (cf. Acts 6:10), nor resist their voice (Jud. 16:14).

6. The Our Father

The Father of the Society: all sons of the same Father, of the Father who asked the Son, loaded with the cross at La Storta, to receive Ignatius as his servant, thereby confirming the name of "Society of Jesus." The *"Our Father"* is the perfect prayer for the individual and for the community.

"Who are in heaven." A Jesuit must always look heavenwards. There is his Father and his fatherland. Our entire life is for the Kingdom. *"Your Kingdom come."* All our labors would be of no avail without the divine help in establishing this Kingdom. The whole Society asks for this grace most earnestly, because it knows that the success of all its undertakings hinges on the answer to the prayer.

"Your will be done." We must cooperate with the divine will, for which it is necessary to know it. Give us, Lord, the sense of true discernment for knowing at every moment what your will for us is. Keep on enlightening us to find your will and strengthening us to fulfill it.

The Society's only goal is the carrying out of your will, your will manifested in various ways but specially through obedience. My responsibility, as superior general of the Society, is very great indeed. To him all authority is given *"ad aedificationem"!* Your will be done: may I never be an obstacle; may I never disfigure, misrepresent or mistake your will for the Society. It is very painful to think that this might happen; keep me faithful to your teaching and never let me be parted from you (prayer before Communion). I consider this a most necessary grace. Therefore, bowing before the paten that holds your Body, I repeat this prayer again and again: death a thousand times rather than to be separated from you. "As the Lord lives. . . wherever my lord the king shall be, whether for death or for life, there also will your servant be" (2 Sam. 15:21).

With my eyes fixed on the consecrated host I present it to the Brother who accompanies me in the celebration and takes the place of all the Jesuits. As the first disciples who saw Jesus when John the Baptist drew their attention to him. . . There they saw a man; here we see only a piece of bread. This is an act of true faith: believing against what we see. The act of faith in the Eucharist is indeed "a hard saying; who can listen to it?" (Jn. 6:60). No, Lord, faith in the Eucharistic mystery is not hard, it is rather a motive of immense joy: "Lord, to whom shall we go? You have the words of eternal life" (Jn. 6:68). I believe!

"Lord, I am not worthy, but only say the word and I shall be healed" (cf. Mt. 8:8), as you healed the centurion's servant. The Society believes that you are the Lord, and want to shelter you under its roof: in our houses, in our churches, in which we want to visit you and contribute to your glorification and cult. And especially the Society wants to shelter you in the hearts of each one of us and in the tabernacle of each community, where they will keep you company and seek from you light, comfort and strength to carry out the mission you have entrusted to them.

Enter, Lord, under the roof of your Society. We need you. There are so many crises of faith, so many sophisticated interpretations parading as scientifically theological...; at times even Christian piety is made light of as though these manifestations of solid and Ignatian faith were antiquated superstitions. "And my soul shall be saved." Lord, do not permit the Society to yield in this matter or degenerate from what St. Ignatius wanted it to be.

Looking fixedly at the white host, I fall on my knees, and 27,000 Jesuits with me, saying as the apostle Thomas from the bottom of my soul and with unswerving faith, "My Lord and my God" (Jn. 20:28).

8. The Body of Christ Keep Me for Everlasting Life

7. The Mass in my Cathedral

Lord, keep the whole Society; keep me especially, since you have given me this office of so great responsibility. Communitarian communion; identification with Christ. A food that is not transformed but transforms. Body of the Society christified; all united and converted into Christ himself. What better "union of hearts!" "For me to live is Christ" (Phil. 1:21), now more than ever.

How well Nadal's observations fit in here! "Accept and diligently exercise the union wherewith the Spirit of the Lord favors you regarding Christ and his powers. Thus you may come to perceive in your soul that you understand through his intellect, will by his will, remember through his memory, and that your entire self, your existence, your life and your actions are realized not in you but in Christ. This is the highest perfection in this life, power divine, happiness beyond compare" (Nadal, MHSI *Orationis Observationes*, n. 308, p. 122).

With this identification of the Society and of each one of the Society with Christ our apostolic activity and our help to souls will gain in efficacy; our words will be those of Christ who knows which is the suitable word at every moment; our plans and manners of apostolate will be precisely those which the Lord will inspire us, which cannot fail to be fruitful. . . a Society of Jesus, truly of Jesus, one with Him.

9. The Blessing of Almighty God

How consoling and moving for me, as identified with Christ, to impart the blessing, his blessing, to the universal Society, a blessing which cannot fail to be efficacious.

This blessing goes to you, workers of the Lord's vineyard, scattered throughout the world and beset with so many difficulties;

—to you, who are bound to the bed of suffering by pain and infirmity, and offer your prayers and afflictions for souls and for the Church and the Society;

—to you, Superiors, who bear a heavy responsibility and have been entrusted with a task not easy in the present times;

—to you, in charge of the formation of our young Jesuits, who are shaping the Society of tomorrow;

—to you, Coadjutor Brothers, who in a decisive moment of our history are going through a profound transformation and who are serving the Church and the Society with so much dedication and selflessness;

—to you, young scholastics and novices, in whom necessarily rests the hope of the Society for the future, for which you ought to be men dedicated to the Church and souls in the Society, deeply imbued with the spirit of St. Ignatius;

—to you very specially, living in countries deprived of true freedom, who need to feel that the Society is very near to you and values your difficult ministry and testimony;

—to all of you, in the furthermost corners of the world, in the most hidden room in our houses, in the remotest station in the jungle:

May the blessing of Almighty God, Father, Son, and Holy Spirit descend upon you and remain with you always.

The Mass in my Cathedral is ended. Go and set the world on fire!

8

A PRAYER TO JESUS CHRIST OUR MODEL

Conclusion of the Address
"Our Way of Proceeding"

Rome
January 18, 1979

At the end of 1979 every Jesuit received a copy of a talk Father Arrupe had given in Rome earlier that year. It was on "Our Way of Proceeding" or the Jesuit Way of Life. As Father General says at the very beginning, "This talk is a further contribution to what I have said on other occasions about the renewal, updating and adaptation of the Society as called for by the last two General Congregations, in implementation of Vatican II."

Among the genuine traits of the Jesuit charism Father Arrupe includes a love for the person of Christ. He says: "Ignatian spirituality is eminently Christocentric. Love for Christ gives unity to everything in the life and work of Ignatius, and in our way of proceeding, for everything is a concrete application of that love on the level of attitudes and actions. Just as everything converges on Christ, so the love for Christ, in Ignatius' intuition, unifies the dialectical pairs into which our apostolic action is diffracted:

—*prayer and action*

—*dedication to the perfection of self and neighbor*

—*use of supernatural and human instruments*

—*pluralism and unity*

—*one's own effort and total dependence on God*
—*poverty and having the most effective means*
—*local insertion and universality."*

"To live that intense love for Christ the person, to aspire to a 'mind of Christ' that will make us be, seem and act like him, is the first and fundamental trait of our way of proceeding. To attain this ideal, St.Ignatius turns to the Mother, so that she will place him with her son."

The conclusion of that discourse, which some think was one of the most important documents of Father Arrupe's generalate, is a typical example of his style of prayers, saturated with the New Testament atmosphere and the spirit of the Jesuit institute, as well as delicately attuned to the contemporary situation. It also brings into relief what the devotion to the Heart of Christ means to every Jesuit.

*

A Prayer to Christ Our Model in the Apostolate

Hebr. 12:2

1 Pet. 1:8

Lord, meditating on "our way of proceeding," I have discovered that the ideal of *our* way of acting is *your* way of acting. For this reason I fix my eyes on you;* the eyes of faith see your face as you appear in the gospel. I am one of those about whom St. Peter says: "You did not see him, yet you love him, and still without seeing him, you are already filled with a joy so glorious that it cannot be described, because you believe."*

Jn. 13:15

1 Cor. 11:1

Lord, you yourself have told us: "I have given you an example to follow."* I want to follow you in that way so that I can say to others: "Be imitators of me a I am of Christ."* Although I am

8. Jesus Christ our Model

not able to mean it as literally as St. John, I would like to be able to proclaim, at least through the faith and wisdom that you give me, what I have heard, what I have seen with my eyes, what I have contemplated and touched with my hands concerning the Word of Life; the Life manifested itself, and I have seen it and give witness.* Although not with bodily eyes, certainly through the eyes of faith.

1 Jn. 1
Cf. Jn. 20 :25–27; 1:14; 15:27 Lk. 24,39

Above all, give me that *sensus Christi** about which St. Paul speaks: that I may feel with your feelings, with the sentiments of your heart, which basically are love for your Father,* and love for mankind.* No one has shown more charity than you, giving your life for your friends* with that *kenosis** of which St. Paul speaks. And I would like to imitate you not only in your feelings but also in—everyday life, acting, as far as possible, as you did.

1 Cor. 2 :16

Jn. 14:31
Jn. 13:1
Jn. 15:13
Phil. 2:7

May I learn from you and from your ways, as St Ignatius did:* how to eat and drink; how to attend banquets;* how to act when hungry or thirsty,* when tired from the ministry* when in need of rest or sleep.*

Mk. 2:16; 3:20   Jn. 4: 31-33

Mt. 9:19; Jn. 2:1;12:2 Lk. 7:16
Mt. 4:2; Jn. 4:7;19:28–30
Jn. 4:6
Mk. 4:38

Lk. 17 :16	Teach me your way of relating to disciples, to sinners, to children,* to Pharisees, Pilates and Herods; also to John the Baptist before his birth* and afterwards in the Jordan.* Teach me how you deal with your disciples, especially the most intimate: with Peter,* with John,* with the traitor Judas.* How delicately you treat them on Lake Tiberias, even preparing breakfast for them! How you washed their feet!
Lk. I :41–45	
Mt. 3: 13.17	
Mt. 10:2–12 Mk. 3:16	
Jn. 19:26–27	
Jn. 13:26 Lk. 22 :48	
Mt. 9:36; 14:14; 15:32; 20:34	Teach me how to be compassionate to the suffering,* to the poor, the blind, the lame, and the lepers; show me how you revealed your deepest emotions, as when you shed tears,* or when you felt sorrow and anguish to the point of sweating blood and needed an angel to console you.* Above all, I want to learn how you supported the extreme pain of the cross, including the abandonment by your Father.*
Lk. 7:13	
Cf. Mt. 9:36; 14:14;15:32; 20:34	
Lk. 7:13; 19:41	
Jn.l 1:33,35,38 Mt. 26:37–39	
Mt. 27:46	

8. Jesus Christ our Model

Your humanity flows out from the gospel, which shows you as noble, amiable, exemplary and sublime, with a perfect harmony between your life and your doctrine. Even your enemies said: "Master we know that you are truthful, that you teach the way of God in truth and care not for any man, for you regard not the person of men."* The gospel shows your virile manner, hard on yourself in privations and wearying work,* but for others full of kindness, with a consuming longing to serve.*

It is true that you were hard on those in bad faith, but your goodness drew the multitudes; the sick and infirm felt instinctively that you would have pity on them;* you so electrified the crowds that they forgot to eat;* with a knowledge of everyday life you could offer parables that everyone understood, parables both vigorous and esthetic. Your friendship was for everyone,* but you manifested a special love for some, like John,* and special friendship for some, like Lazarus Martha and Mary.* Show me how you expressed joy at festive gatherings; for example, at Cana.*

Mt. 22:16

Mt. 8:20

Mt. 20:28 Cfr. Phil. 2:7

Mt. 9:36

Mt. 14:16

Jn. 15:15
Jn. 13:23;19:26

Jn. 11:36

Jn. 2:1

You were in constant contact with you Father in prayer, and your formal prayer often lasting all night, was certainly a source of the luminous transcendence noticed by your contemporaries.* Your presence instilled respect, consternation trembling, admiration, and sometimes even profound fear from various types and classes of people.

<small>Mk. 1:35, Cfr. Mt. 14:23; 26:36
Lk. 5:16; 6:12; 9:18;11:1</small>

Teach me your way of looking at people: as you glanced at Peter after his denial,* as you penetrated the heart of the rich young man* and the hearts of your disciples.*

<small>Lk. 22:61
Mk. 10:21
Mk. 10:23; 3:34; 5:31–32</small>

I would like to meet you as you really are, since your image changes those with whom you come into contact. Remember John the Baptist's first meeting with you.* And the centurion's feeling of unworthiness* and the amazement of all those who saw miracles and other wonders.* How you impressed your disciples,* the rabble in the Garden of Olives,* Pilate* and his wife* and the centurion at the foot of the cross.*

<small>Mt. 3: 14
Mt. 8:9

Mt. 8:27;9:33 Mk. 5: 15; 7:37
Lk. 4:36; 5:26
Mk. 1:27 Mt. 13:54
Jn. 18:6 Jn. 19:8 Mt. 27:19
Lk. 23:47</small>

The same Peter who was vividly impressed by the miraculous catch of fish also felt vividly the tremendous distance between himself, a sinner, and you. He and the other Apostles were overcome with fear.*

<small>Lk. 5:8–9</small>

8. Jesus Christ our Model

Jn. 6:35–39 Mt. 5:2

Mt. 7:29 Lk. 4:22

Jn. 7:46

I would like to hear and be impressed by your manner of speaking, listening, for example, to your discourse in the synagogue in Capernaum* or the Sermon on the Mount, where your audience felt you "taught as one who has authority" and not as the Scribes.*

In the words of grace that came from your mouth the authority of the Spirit of God was evident.* No one doubted that the superhuman majesty came from a close bond between Jesus and God. We have to learn from you the secret of such a close bond or union with God: in the more trivial, everyday actions, with that total dedication to loving the Father and all humanity, the perfect *kenosis* at the service of others, aware of the delicate humanity that makes us feel close to you and of that divine majesty that makes us feel so distant from such grandeur.

I beg Mary, your Most Holy Mother who contributed so much to your formation and way of acting, to help me and all sons of the Society to become her sons, just like you, born of her and living with her all the days of your life.

PART TWO

Today's Theology on the Heart of Christ

9

THE HEART OF CHRIST
CENTER OF THE CHRISTIAN MYSTERY
AND KEY OF THE UNIVERSE

Chapter of a Book Published in 1981

This article, dated January 6, 1989, was published in English as a chapter of a book, titled "With a Human Heart."

This book is a symposium edited by Father E. J. Cuskelly, M.S.C., Superior General in Rome of the Missionaries of the Sacred Heart, who requested the contributions from competent writers. After publication of the book he wrote in 1981: "I got my great friend Father Arrupe to write one chapter of the book." Some of the articles of this book are very scholarly and others are pastorally oriented. (The book can be purchased from the publisher, Chevalier Press, I Roma Avenue, Kensington 2033, Australia.)

The National Director of the Apostleship of Prayer in India, Fr. Paul Wenisch S.J., found the chapter so good that he reprinted it and sent a copy of it to each Jesuit in India. This is probably the most complete synthesis of the theological thought of Father Arrupe on the Sacred Heart.

The Missionaries of the Sacred Heart are a congregation of priests and brothers founded at Issoudun, France, in 1854 by Father Jules Chevalier. His first purpose was to renew the faith, especially in France, through devotion to the Sacred Heart, but his foundation soon grew also into a worldwide missionary institute. The Congregation has a province in the United States with headquarters near Chicago in Aurora, Illinois. They hope to open some missions in India.

We are grateful to Father Cuskelly, at present Auxiliary Bishop of Brisbane, for giving us permission to reprint the chapter of Father Arrupe, whom he knew in Rome as a fellow member of the Union of Superiors General of Religious Men. The present editor had the honor of doing some secretarial work for him during the Bishops' Synod in Rome in October 1980.

I. THE HEART IS THE CENTER

Richness of the Word "Heart"

1. The word "heart," both in everyday language and in Biblical terminology is one of those words which K. Rahner has called an *Urwort,* that is a root-word, a parent-word which generates other words. Such words are packed with meaning and are very difficult to define, and for that reason are also highly evocative. Just as a small sea conch conjures up the roar and fury of the sea, such words stir up a rich variety of ideas and sentiments. The word "mother" is another example. Who can say all that this word evokes? Or who can reduce it to a definition? To any definition of this word one can say "yes, all that but more," because no one can reach the very depth of its meaning and even less communicate it to others. The value of these words is precisely that we can understand each other's meaning when we refer to deep and complex realities. The psychology of language has in such words a subject for absorbing research.

2. But the very richness and depth of these words is, in part, their weakness. They are used so much in human communication that they become victims of abuse and end up cheapened and corrupted, or else they are watered-down so that they lose their flavor, or again they are inflated and adapted to the fleeting fancy of the current vogue, then discarded abruptly. Fortunately nature always wins out, and these words—which instead of a human figment seem a divine gift—come to life again and bloom, their profound meaning and values intact.

3. "Heart of Jesus" is an expression that has suffered such vicissitudes. Marked with the symbolism and with the literary style

9. Center of the Christian Mystery

and imagery of an era—which is necessarily fleeting—it seemed that it would remain buried beneath the wave of renewal. Not for long. "Heart of Christ" is a phrase of unusual aptness and so rooted in biblical meaning that it is irreplaceable. It was sufficient to free it of superficial connotations for the original, rich and mysterious meaning to be restored. Heart of Jesus: all the love of Christ, God and man, sent by the Father, through the Spirit, who offers himself in redemption for all and with each of us establishes a personal relationship.

4. "... the inner mystery of man, in Biblical and non-Biblical language is expressed by the word 'heart.' Christ, the Redeemer of the world, is the one who penetrated in a unique unrepeatable way the mystery of man and entered his 'heart'" *(Redemptor Hominis* 8). "In him human nature, by the very fact that it was assumed, not absorbed, has been raised in us also to a dignity beyond compare. By his incarnation, the Son of God has in a certain way united himself with each man. He worked with human hands, he thought with a human mind. He acted with a human will, and with a human heart the loved" (G.S. 22).

The Love of the Heart of Christ—Key to the Understanding of the History of Salvation

5. This gift which the Father has given us in the person of Christ is our salvation, the salvation of all men. Christ in his incarnation intervenes in the established relationship of man with God and completely transforms it. The great power which effects this revolution, the great novelty of the New Alliance is the love of his heart, and the love which He comes to kindle in each one of us. He has sealed this New Alliance with the sacrifice of reconciliation offered once and renewed in each Eucharistic celebration, a sacrifice completely acceptable and pleasing to the Father and gloriously sublimated in his Resurrection.

6. The pristine catechesis and the Gospels derived from it are the story of this love. The four Gospels show us this love in action. This is especially true of the last chapters of St. John's Gospel and of his letters—very particularly his first letter where the theme of love becomes an exhortation, divine-human coherence: a person completely dedicated to pointing us directly to the feelings and

sentiments of the Heart of Christ and urging us to reciprocate his love.

Paul, for his part, spreads the Good News throughout the whole world to all men, the news of our new condition, that we are a "new creature." The old law has been abrogated by God's love. In this way the fourth Gospel and the *"corpus paulinum"* marvelously complement and shed light on each other.

7. If the Old Testament is in essence the history of human tension in the presence of God the Creator and can be summed up in the counterposition: "heart of stone"/"new heart," the New Testament is summed up in the new relationship of love: *"cor Christi/cor Hominis,"* (Heart of Christ/heart of man). Thus, a term which is so typical in Semitic languages is raised in the New Testament message to a much higher level of meaning: the sentiments and acts of the Son of God and of each person in their reciprocal relationship.

Christ, Defined by His Heart

8. It is impossible to find in the New Testament a word which more readily and accurately, more profoundly and with more human warmth, could come close to a definition of the person of Christ than his "Heart." Much of what John thinks and says of Christ is contained in the word "logos," but there are many passages that do not fit that concept and also much of what the synoptics say is not contained in it; apart, of course, from the human characteristics which her and there bear out the rich personality of Christ. The word "logos" has a mental resonance that does not immediately "describe" Christ. Rarely, on the other hand, do the Gospel reveal some interior characteristic of Christ that we cannot epitomize in his heart. Furthermore, the external signs, his parables and discourses, his whole life as presented in the Gospels—even considered as "Kerygma"—are not totally the Mission received from the Father. And it is understood or understandable in all their profound meaning unless they are read from the angle of his heart. Read in this light, on the other hand, Jesus is seen whole and undivided in each moment of his life. All that He says and does in any instance gives us the measure of his inner being, of his infinite precisely these inner depths of Christ's life and being that we must try to discover through his words and deeds.

9. Consequently, it is not old-fashioned piety which makes us refer to the heart of Christ in order to sum up in one word all the values which we find in his person. There is no other expression more apt to convey "the breadth and the length, the height and the depth (of) the love of Christ, which is beyond all knowledge" (Eph. 3:18). Neither the "logos" of John, nor Wisdom, nor Son of Man, nor Messiah. Not even the definitions which Jesus applied metaphorically to himself: way, truth, life, light, good shepherd, bread, etc. Jesus himself, when he wanted to describe himself and his deepest sentiments, put aside all metaphors and used simple everyday language: "learn from me, for I am gentle and humble in heart" (Mt. 11:29).

Christ Values the Heart of Each Man

10. Christ judges each man by his heart. It is true to say that in the teaching of the Prophets interior dispositions are already given considerable relevance; Jeremiah (4:1–4 and passim) and especially Ezekiel, and also that marvel, the language of the convert in Psalm 51, the *Miserere*. John the Baptist centers his preaching on the same theme and with the same stress as the prophets. Jesus also will do so but if, before, love was implied in the sorrow of contrition ("crushing" of the heart), in the preaching of Jesus it is the other way round: it is remorse that is implied in love.

11. For Christ a man's coherence and integrity is of the essence. If there is one thing that really drives Jesus to holy indignation it is pharisaic insincerity, duplicity of heart, palming off the appearance of righteousness for love. Christ insists again and again that the goodness or badness of man is in his heart. The exaltation of man's inner being stresses a line along which the prophets had hardly advanced at all, namely, that it depends on man's inner self whether he is able to be incorporated into God's Kingdom. The Old Testament image of the Kingdom is now definitively replaced.

It is in the heart of man that, once the divine filiation is restored, the union between man and God is accomplished. The kingdom, before its eschatological completion, is nothing else but the *"ekklesia,"* the community of those who through faith have received this interior transformation (cf. 1 Cor. 1:2) and in brotherly union are on their way to the Father's house.

12. The central point in the relationship *heart of Christ/heart of man* is love. More than faith, more than any other sentiment, it is love which transcendentally describes man and it is also love which comes closest to a definition of God. God is love. Christ corresponds to the Father's infinite love with absolute loving obedience, and at the same time he loves man "to the end" (Jn. 13:1). Christ's heart is the smelting vessel of his love for the Father as Word and as man, and also of his love for mankind. In the heart of man redeemed by Christ this love must find a proportionate response. This precisely is Paul's claim: "He loved me and sacrificed himself for my sake" (Gal. 2: 20). In the one divine person of Christ the two natures establish an encounter of love.

II. Christ: A New Concept of Love

The Love of Yahweh in the Old Testament

13. From the beginning God took the initiative in dialogue of love with man. But one cannot say that man completely understood or corresponded to the divine initiative, Biblical man "knew" God, and for a Semite to know something is to have a certain experience of it, and in some way to love it. In the earlier period, the idea of God as creator paramount; God mysterious and distant who chose his friends and confidants among men: the prophets and patriarchs. They are the witnesses of the drama of Yahweh's love and wrath. The people respond with adoration and obedience. Many of the Psalms both before and after the exile show that not only the people as a group of their leaders, but each individual and in particular each "poor" one, each "little" one, each "just" one is loved by God.

14. But there are many questions still left unanswered. In what way is Yahweh's love interpreted? How does one respond to it? What is the relationship between the love of Yahweh and the love of one's neighbor? Yahweh is accepted as the one God, the creator, the protector, the one who mysteriously rewards the righteous. His love is made tangible in his offer of the alliance by which he weds himself to his chosen people. Israel's response can be nothing else but submission and fidelity, obedience to the law. This would be the meaning of the first precept of the decalogue: love God "with all your heart, with all your soul, with all your strength" (Deut. 6:5).

Even the Song of Songs, after all, is just a poetic exaltation of the alternate searching and possessing of Yahweh and his people. Parallel to the prophetic line which presents the alliance as a relationship of love, there is the legal line, which eventually predominates and increasingly insists on interpreting the alliance in terms of accepting the law and obeying it: a law that becomes fragmented in countless precepts; an oppressive law which just about smothers love. Love of Yahweh turns into fear of Yahweh. The center of gravity, so to speak, moves from the cordial to the servile. This fact provokes Christ's bitter reproaches against the Pharisees.

15. And perhaps it could not have been otherwise, since the revelation of the Trinity was yet to come. Love could not be perfect as long as men did not know God as Father, and were unaware of their kinship with the Son, and had not received the Spirit. And how could they have anticipated, Yahweh's personal intervention in the history of his people by becoming one of them? Their idea of the Messiah was clouded by these obscurities. They expected a regal Messiah, a priestly Messiah and, above all, a deliverer. The Messiah's relationship to God was still ill-defined and there was hardly an inkling of what his relationship to mankind would be. The veil which hid the mystery of the Trinity during the time of the Promise also concealed the fullness of God's love. The plurality of Persons was vague, barely a metaphoric intuition and therefore the One Sent could hardly be identified with one of these Persons. Furthermore the notion that the Chosen One should suffer and die was a scandal to the Jews. One can say that they were not ready for such love, for such overwhelming love. Christ, defined by his heart, surpasses all the expectations of the Old Testament and is established as the key to the whole history of salvation.

The Love of Neighbor in the Old Testament

16. The Old Testament also enjoins love of one's neighbor, but with obscure restrictions. True, the book of Leviticus completes the commandment about loving God with "a second commandment":

"You must love your neighbor as yourself" (Lv. 19:18) and "you must love the stranger as yourself" (Lv. 19:34) but "neighbor" is practically the same as "brother," that is to say, those who belong to the predestined race. Especially after the Exile, brotherhood has well recognized limits. The stranger who must be loved is a stranger (foreigner) happening by, or a resident: "for you were strangers in the land of Egypt," (Deut. 10: 19) but it excludes the gentiles who by definition are enemies of God and consequently enemies of his people. The question "who is my neighbor?" does not have a clear-cut answer, even for a well-intentioned Israelite. The less well-intentioned can give all sorts of wrong answers. Our Lord gives his own clear reply to this question in the parable of the "Good Samaritan" (Lk. 10: 25–37).

17. The worst kind of hatred is hatred for religious motives. It is so much easier to justify when it appears under the guise of zeal and pious outrage. If even Yahweh could become an enemy of his unfaithful people and punish them and make them suffer, is an Israelite's hatred for a heathen, or a dissident or a public sinner not justified also? The pathetic exhibition of his hatred for sin comes to be regarded as religious fervor and so the contest is on: who can voice the most bloodcurdling curses? From simply keeping one's distance from the "impure," or refusing to have dealings with a dissident (e.g. Samaritans) or tearing one's robes in outrage at a blasphemer, they reach the extreme vengeance of stoning to death.

Christ, Sign of the Love of the Father

18. God in the Old Testament shows his love for man by his predilection for a particular people. He establishes an alliance with it, he gives it a promised land, he leads it back there after various exiles. It is a story of tormented love. But in the fullness of time the love of the Father for mankind takes on a completely new expression in an unrepeatable gesture: his Son is "sent" to be the protagonist on earth in the drama of this love-dialogue between God and man. This sending of the Son completes all the most loving gestures of the time of the promises... "the promises God made, the Yes to them all is in Him" (2 Cor. I:20). "In Him, the love God has for us was made manifest" (Rom. 8:39). The initiative for this new order is exclusively divine and has no other explanation but love: "God's love for us was revealed when God sent into the world his only Son.

.. This is the love I mean: not our love for God but God's love for us when he sent his Son" (John 4: 9ss.).

19. In this way, the love of God is manifested no longer through actions alone but through a divine Person who, by the very act of his Incarnation in the nature of man, shows concretely the heights of this love. In Christ, God loves man infinitely and is loved by Him. That is why Christ proves the genuineness of his being sent by the Father, not so much by his omnipotence, his signs, or his omniscience, as by his radically new concept of love which he comes to promulgate and to exemplify. The qualitative leap from the love enjoined in the Old Testament to the love envisioned by Christ affects love of God as well as love of one's neighbor. Through the revelation of his divine nature and through the acceptance of his supreme sacrifice, Christ opens man's eyes to the reality of God's infinite and pure love which to redeem us and return us to our former estate as his sons "did not spare his own Son, but offered him for all of us" (Rom. 8:32). "Christ ... loved us and gave himself up in our place" (Eph. 5:2). It is a love which is related to the alliance established in the Old Testament only in as much as it is the consummation of the promise.

20. In reference to fraternal love and universal charity, the qualitative leap introduced by Christ is equally unprecedented. The novelty consists in the cancellation of all restrictions in the concept of neighbor and in the heightening and sublimation of the motive for charity. That the exterior acts by which this charity is expressed must be of unrestricted generosity is an obvious consequence. But before analyzing these concepts it will be well to call attention to two fundamental considerations.

Christ is Bearer of the Father's Love

21. The first point to consider is the clear consciousness that Jesus has of the innovative character of the love he promulgates: He is fully aware that by so doing he is transcending the law and the prophets and is declaring his messianic role. In the doctrinal summary which Matthew gives in chapters 5 to 7 of his gospel, no less than six times Jesus introduces his perceptive teaching with a formula brimming with meaning: "You have learned how it was

said to our ancestors. . . But I say this to you . . ." (Mt. 5: 21, 27, 31, 33, 38, 43). There is no doubt that, however much this striking repetition can be ascribed to Semitic taste, it is also the true echo of the emphatic will of Christ that he be understood regarding the innovative character of his doctrine and that effectively He is placing himself above the law. Three of the precepts thus solemnly promulgated concern charity. The striking attitude Christ shows in this connection is paralleled only by his vehemence abolishing divorce. When Christ at the end of his life will have fully revealed at its deepest level all his understanding of love, he will affirm unequivocally that this is a "new" commandment (Jn. 13:14) as is also "new" the alliance sealed with his blood which will be shed for us (Lk. 22:20) as the supreme truth of his love. So unexpected is this novelty that at the beginning of his preaching his hearers exclaimed "What is this? This is a new doctrine with authority behind it" (Mk. 1:27). Love is the most radiant novelty of the Gospel: it is preeminently the commandment which the Lord chose to call "mine" (Jn. 15:12).

Only One Love

22. The second consideration is this: The reason for loving one's neighbor is a theological reason which closely relates it to the love of God. They are not two parallel loves, nor is love of neighbor a subordinate love. It is the two sides of one love, as one is the love within the Trinity and one the love with which Christ loves the Father and mankind. The close connection of the second commandment to the first (as we shall see later, in Paul's and John's description it acquires its highest expression) conforms to this profound causality: one cannot love God without loving one's brother and he who for God loves his brothers is already loving God (cf. Mk. 5: 45 and Lk. 6: 35).

23. The three synoptics report instances when Christ likens love of neighbor to love of God. In Matthew (22: 34–40) and in Mark (12: 28–34), Christ answers the Pharisee's provocative question and with a hint of challenge he blends both commandments into one. In Luke (10: 25ff) it is a quibbling lawyer who has to respond to Christ's sparring question. The casuist links the precept in Deuteronomy (6: 5) about the love of God with that of Leviticus (19:8) about the love of one's neighbor—neighbor of course, as the lawyer understands the

word. To correct the notion, Jesus tells him the parable of the Good Samaritan.

Christ Manifests His Own Love

24. Of nothing else did Christ speak so much as of love, with the exception perhaps of the kingdom: "the kingdom of Heaven is like. . ." But even the parables of the kingdom are set in a context of love. Love with all its harmonics—friendship, compassion, tolerance, benevolence, mercy, sadness, hope, joy, etc.—is enough to describe Christ in his inner self, in his heart. Christ calls his followers to goodness and love, sometimes directly, from the beatitudes right up to the sermon of the last supper; at other times indirectly and through sublime allegories: the Prodigal Son, the Lost Pearl, the Stray Sheep and the whole cycle of the Good Shepherd parables. Christ "goes about doing good" (Acts 10:38) and displays his miraculous power in "signs" which are more often acts of kindness than proofs of his messiahship.

Love Without Bounds: Universal

25. If the love which Christ practices and teaches is the radically new feature of the Gospel, as indicated earlier, it is because it formally suppresses and abolishes the limitations and restrictions which previously narrowed down the idea of love. We know that "Love your neighbor as yourself" (Lv. 19: 18) is already the second commandment in the Old Law. But one needs only to compare this text with the other in which the first commandment is promulgated (Deut. 6: 4–9), to appreciate the difference in emphasis between the two commandments. The concept of neighbor is vague. The fluctuating meaning of the Old Testament expressions—"the other," "the brother"—is an example of this vagueness. When the Decalogue, promulgated in other texts (Ex. 20: 2–17, and Deut. 5: 6–12) is epitomized in a single sentence (Deut. 6:5), all mention of love of neighbor disappears: "You shall love Yahweh your God with all your heart, with all your soul, with all your strength." There is no mention of neighbor whatsoever.

26. Christ breaks down the fences of a restricted brotherhood, and this is his great revolution of love: universal salvation, universal filiation, universal brotherhood and universal love, are all correlative ideas logically connected and interchangeable. We will

see that there is only one exception: the preference for the neediest.

27. But it is necessary to mention expressly the two most radical changes introduced by Christ in the notion of universal love. In this new vision no one at all is excluded, not even those falling within the two categories which the law excepted and religiously set apart: the enemy and the sinner. The whole history of Israel is a struggle for survival. Hatred for one's enemy is even ranked as a religious sentiment and as such it is expressed even in the sacred books (Psalms 137, 139 etc.). Enmity toward a personal enemy, a thief and those who ensnare the just man, is lawful. It is already an advance in moderating revenge when it is stipulated that retaliation must not exceed the offence: "You have learned that it was said: 'eye for eye and tooth for tooth!' But I say this to you..." (Mk. 5:38; Lk. 6:27). Jesus is specific: "Love your enemies, do good to those who hate you, bless those who curse you, pray for those who mistreat you." This is one of the high points of the Gospel, because here we discover the essence of Christianity: unconditional fraternal love.

28. Jesus expressed his thoughts in semitic imagery: lend the other cheek, give your cloak as well as your tunic, go the extra mile. The conclusion of the text is of the highest importance because Jesus gives the reason for his precept: "So that you will be sons of the Heavenly Father, for he is kind even to the ungrateful and the wicked." The image which Jesus gives us of the Father is no longer that of the God who inspires revenge but of a Father whose perfection is manifested in his mercy. All is contained and epitomized in this lofty exhortation: "You must therefore be perfect just as your heavenly Father perfect" (Mt. 5:48). What reversal of values could be imagined more radical than this? Now it is the enemy that has to be loved, and precisely because this is God's way.

Love of Sinners

29. There is still more: one has to love God's enemy, the sinner. Scripture praised the hatred God shows toward idolatry, plunder, perjury, any kind of sin (cf. Deut. 12:31; Jer. 44:, Zech. 8:17; Prov. 5:16) and consequently for the sinner who in a way is one with his sin, and can be chastised with an impure illness. The Israelite affirms his piety by hating sinners. And here is Jesus declaring he has come not for the just but for them (Mk. 2:17).

9. Center of the Christian Mystery

Taking his place in the line of teacher-prophets, Jesus, as his forerunner, announces the Good News for sinners disposed to repent. In Jesus, denunciation of sin rivals his inexhaustible compassion for the sinner. Jesus causes scandal when he forgives the adulteress, when he speaks to the samaritan woman, when he heals and pardons paralytics and the possessed, when he ignores legal impurity in order to share a meal with sinners. To describe the Father and himself, in the parables of the Prodigal Son and of the Good Shepherd, Jesus refers to his heart open to forgive. By his whole life and by his death he will confirm all he has preached. He will even call his betrayer friend and ask forgiveness for those who are crucifying him.

30. More than his parables it is Christ's life that launches this revolution of love. Samaritans, gentiles of Cana, Tyre or Sidon, officials of the Roman occupation, publicans, prostitutes, lepers, all have a place in his heart. To love sinners Christ throws down the barriers of legal impurities, of the sabbath observance, of religious discrimination, of the sacredness of temple offerings. Loving sinners, Christ strips hatred of its last pretext: religious zeal.

The Supreme Love of the Heart of Christ

31. It might seem that nothing could be added to Christ's proclamation of universal love made at the beginning' of his ministry, and of which his whole life has been a constant confirmation. All the aspects of love are illustrated: the love of God whom he taught us to call "Father," the love of himself and the love of our brothers. But Christ reserved for the last hour—and this word can be taken in the Johannine sense—the deepest and most meaningful lesson of his pedagogy of love. As evening falls, the day before his passion, and time is running out, when he no longer needs to hold bat from revealing the fullness of his heart, now that his disciples have been witnesses of his life and work and are soon to be witnesses of his sacrifice, Jesus discloses to them the wealth of sublime reasons on which his love for them is based and which must inspire the love they bear for each other.

32. "Love one another; just as I have loved you" (Jn. 13:34). With good reason Christ can describe this commandment as new, for new indeed is such an unimaginable reach of love. "You must love your neighbor as yourself. I am Yahweh" (Lev. 19:18). The scope of pre-Christian love, which could have been as an ideal, in this new light shows its inadequacy. "As I have loved you." This comparison is the ever pressing goad that from that time onward urges each believer in Christ to strive to love his neighbor without reservations or hesitations. It is a goal to which we must aspire always, even though we know we will never be able to reach it. Only "through his Spirit for your inner self to grow strong... planted in love and built on love, will you grasp the breadth and the length, the height and the depth of the love of Christ, which is beyond all knowledge" (Eph. 3: 17–19).

33. "As I have loved you" contains the entire mystery of the Incarnation, the *"kenosis"* accepted as preparation for the Paschal Mystery, the gift of self in the Eucharist, the consummation of his sacrifice and his perpetual intercession before the Father. Jesus speaks as a man to that puny flock of fearful men, but his words echo the love of God. The ultimate clue to this love beyond belief will be his twofold standard.

34. Christ proclaims a new comparative standard of love and he will personally fulfill it, "a man can have no greater love than to lay down his life for his friends" (Jn. 15:13). Less than a day before his death, these words are evidence of a supreme love; it is the measure of his love for them and thus the measure of love which they must have for each other. Love is measured by self-giving. Jesus faces death and accepts, I conscious of the fact that by his death he proclaims his love for all men. The disciples will eventually understand the full value of the comparison "as I have loved you": dying for you.

35. The second standard is by appeal to a mystery "As the Father has loved me, so I have loved you" (Jn. 15:9). Christ will repeat this in nearly the same words a few moments later in the priestly prayer; "I have loved them as you have loved me." Words which must be received with a reverence beyond expression. The whole heart of Jesus pours itself out in this supreme confidence that surpasses any human measure, because it already points to the infinite love within

the Trinity: the mutual love of Father and Son. But this is the measure of love to which we are urged: love one another as I have loved you, I have loved you as the Father loves me. The most radical innovation the Gospel offers, charity, is thus established in its ultimate expression. But, is it not an exaggeration? No, it is not. Quite the contrary. It is a deliberate and conscious affirmation which John once again puts on the lips of Jesus as the conclusion of the long discourse, just before the evangelist begins the story of the Passion: "that the love with which you loved me may be in them, and so that I may be in them" (Jn. 17: 26).

36. The insertion of the Father as the point of reference for the love between Christ and mankind at this peak moment of the revelation of love is extremely enlightening. The mission of Christ, besides other things, is the revelation of the Father. For this reason it is important to establish that the Fatherhood is also exercised in love, love of the Son, and unmediated love of the Father for mankind. The same Father, whom Christ invoked in the agony in the Garden and on the Cross, the ultimate challenges in the test of his love, is also invoked in the proclamation of fraternal charity. "The Father loves me because I lay down my life in order to take it up again" (Jn. 10:17). The same Father who "... loved the world so much that he gave his only Son, so that everyone who believes in him may not be lost" (Jn. 3:16). Fraternal charity, lived as Christ teaches us, is a direct way to approach the Trinity.

III. The Two Old Precepts Are One

Christ in Our Brothers

37. In love thus understood the unification of the two ancient precepts reaches its highest perfection. Now there is one and no more. The same charity that draws us to God must also bring us closer to our brothers. In them we must find God. Christ is in them, above all in the most needy; in the poor, in the little ones (Mt. 25:40). During his whole life Christ showed his predilection for them and following his example we too must give preference to them. If the discourse on love is reported at the end of John's Gospel just before Christ's passion, it is in the same sequence that Matthew's Gospel reports Christ's proclamation of his identification with the poor. It is as if he were

going out of his way to make sure the fact remains imprinted in our minds: "in so far as you did this to one of the least of these brothers of mine (hungry, thirsty, naked, homeless, sick, oppressed) you did it to me" (Mt. 25:40–45). A love of God that does not find expression in love for mankind is always suspect. Because "a man who does not love the brother that he can see cannot love God, whom he has never seen" (1 Jn. 4:20). John warns us in no uncertain terms that love of God which is not accompanied by love of neighbor is an illusion. His language, which in points is nearly of a gnostic loftiness, becomes concrete and incisive to assert that such love would be inconsistent "if a man who was rich enough in this world's goods saw that one of his brothers was in need, but closed his heart to him, how would the love of God be live in him?" (1 Jn. 3:17). "Closed his heart" means depriving him of the love and the sharing which love implies. Because there is no other word which points more directly to love than the word "heart."

38. Paul, after his conversion will completely assimilate this doctrine. He is the author of the most beautiful hymn to the love of Christ (Rom. 8:31ff), and of the vibrating eulogy of charity (1 Cor. 13). He is the promoter of mutual aid among the churches.

Of this assistance, given in the name of love, he makes an instrument of unity when there is a threat of division between the churches of the Jewish tradition and those burgeoning among the Gentiles (Gal. 1:10; Rom. 15: 26; 1 Cor. 16: 1–4). Two whole chapters of his second letter to the Corinthians are dedicated to organizing, urging and giving meaning to the collection of voluntary offerings (2 Cor. 8 and 9). So impassioned is Paul's plea that, with a hyperbole, he goes so far as to claim that the whole law comes down to fraternal charity, "the whole law is contained in this one command: love your neighbor as yourself" (Gal. 5:14). It is the old formula of Leviticus, brief and incisive, reflecting its rabbinical origin, and it helps him encourage the churches of the diaspora to practice mutual love: "Serve each other for love" (see the same exhortation in Rom. 13: 9–10).

39. St. James, with the semitic expressions which are peculiar to his style, more homiletic than epistolary, exalts the poor and severely chides the rich. Charity must be shown in works so that faith may not become fruitless.

9. Center of the Christian Mystery

Charity and Fullness

40. It is clear that, *"pleroma"* (fullness) is a fundamental concept in Paul's theology. Besides the fullness of the times there is the fullness which dwells in Christ, and again the Church is the fullness of Christ. This great concept is seen throughout Paul's letters, above all in his more lyrical and syntactically more intricate passages, when his enthusiasm for Christ, for the Church or for a particular community, touches off his genius for soaring expressions to convey his thought. In the idea which Paul has of the fullness of Christ and of the Church, love is a basic ingredient. It is not only that love is the dominant theme in the whole divine plan of salvation, that which establishes the harmony of its different aspects: but the fullness of Christ, in whom the Father has placed all things, and the fullness of the Church as mystical body of Christ. "Before the world was made, he chose us in Christ, to be holy and spotless, and to live through love in his presence" (Eph. I:4). It is the love of God which chooses us and to this love corresponds "the love we have for God that has been poured into our hearts by the Spirit which has been given us" (Rom. 5:5). Theologically and anthropologically speaking, the lyrical lift of Paul's hymn to charity (I Cor. 13) marvelously heightens the sweeping novelty of the Gospel: the manifestation of the love of Christ's heart which establishes new relationships between God and man and between man and man.

41. John expounds the same doctrine. He takes it directly from Christ's lips when at the last supper Jesus proclaims his love for us and says that his love is to be the gauge of the love the brethren must have for each other. It seems he is acquitting himself of the last responsibility left before his mission is definitively accomplished: "I have told you this so that my own joy," (this is the messianic joy of the Son of God) "may be in you and your joy be complete" (Jn. 15:11); "while still in the world I have told you these things to share my joy with you to the full" (Jn. 17:13). The fullness of joy of Jesus of which John was a witness is also a sentiment that John repeatedly made his own when he communicated his testimony "We are writing this to you to make our own joy complete" (1 Jn. 1:4). John knows that brothers' love for each other fills Christ's heart

with joy and that sharing in this joy and generating it in the hearts of those who believe in Him is a pre-announcement of the fullness of fruition that those in the Kingdom will enjoy when they will be assumed into the glory of the Father and their human love will be anchored in the infinite love of the Trinity.

There, one will experience that "God is love, and everyone who loves... because God is love... is begotten by God and knows God" (1 Jn. 4:8,16). To be of God and to know God, in John's language, is a way of being possessed by Him and possessing Him. Human love has its point of origin and destiny in the love of the Trinity. There is no higher summit than this.

42. It is now twenty centuries since the promulgation of the one and only commandment of love, a commandment that continues to urge us. Fraternal love continues to be a necessity for all men and for all times, and still more necessary in our time now that the world has become a "global village" and human interchange is on a truly universal scale. Universal brotherhood is no longer a qualitative aspect of love, in the sense of excluding prerequisites. It is a quantitative reality since the revolution brought on by communications, technology, and the possibility of exchanging resources.

Because of this we can no longer plead ignorance of the miseries of our brothers in any part of the world; we can no longer say that they are no responsibility of ours.

43. All the modern tragedies are ultimately a wounding of love or a challenge to our capacity to love. The tragic fratricidal hatred of Cain for Abel is still casting its shadow over us. "This is the message as you heard it from the beginning that we are to love one another; not to be like Cain, who belonged to the Evil One and cut his brother's throat" (1 Jn. 3:11–12), but "this has taught us love that Jesus gave up his life for us; and we, too, ought to give up our lives for our brothers" (ibid. 16).

The Danger of the Old Division

44. For this reason we cannot but decry the emergence of the old Jewish dichotomy which traced a boundary line between love of God and love of one's neighbor; a dissociation *"contra naturam"*

that the Heart of Christ wanted to remedy for all time. It would be going back on the Gospel. We do not have true and full love of God if we do not also manifest it toward our brothers, concretely toward those in whom Christ said we should recognize Him. Nor do we have true and full love of our brothers if in them we fail to see and recognize God and so reduce charity to the level of philanthropy, robbing it of its transcendental dimension. Any of these failings would mean forgetting that "the fundamental law of human perfection, and consequently of the transformation of the world, is the new commandment of love" (G.S. 38; cf. also n. 24). All the excesses of a reductive horizontalism or an unincarnate verticalism are an option between the "first and principal commandment" and the "second which is equal to the first," which after the discourse at the last supper no longer makes sense. They are a fatal corruption of, the model of love proclaimed by Christ.

45. And unfortunately this is the way one could summarize the theoretical ends of the diverging lines of current thought and of Christian action. One must not so exalt Jesus the man, the person who had a predilection for the poor and the simple, who argued for detachment from worldly goods, who was persecuted by the religious and civic structures of his time, that one disregards Christ, the son of the Father, who came into this world to save us all from sin, to infuse into our hearts the love of the Father and to give us the certainty of future life. Neither must one center one's attention on the primacy of faith, on grace, and on the spiritual nature of the kingdom to such an extent that one does not hear with all due sensitivity the cry of the poor, and does not realize what existential human miseries so often challenge fraternal love. So the attitudes are typical of a harmful reductivism. Jesus is indeed the ideal model of a "man for others" who was deeply pained when it happened that his hearers went without eating for three days in order to follow him. (How his heart would suffer today in the face of the widespread and persistent phenomenon of hunger!) But he is above all else Jesus Christ, who "loves us and has washed away our sins with his blood" (Rev. 1:5).

Experience and Knowledge of Christ

46. The cause of this dichotomy, or to put it in more pragmatic terms, of this meaningless fragmentation of the Christ of the Gospels is certainly the fact that we are not fully aware through

experience and knowledge of the many facets of "the love of God which has been poured into our hearts by the Holy Spirit given us" (Rom. 5: 5). Our heart is in danger of continuing to be "hardened" like that of Israel under the alliance. We need that "circumcision of heart" (Rom. 2:29) that frees us from the old alliance of subjection so that we can enter into the new alliance of love. Only this awareness and lived experience of Christ, in faith and charity, will enable us to present to our brothers Christ whole and not mutilated. We can do this only if we have obtained "the spirit of wisdom and perception of what is revealed, to bring [us] to full knowledge of him who enlightens the eyes of [our] mind" (Eph. 1:17–18). Only from Him, in whom abides the fullness of divine life—and not from theorizers or from any power of this world—can we receive that life and lead our brothers in the fullness of the whole Christ, which is the Church.

47. A well-known saying of K. Barth is "Tell me what your Christology is and I will tell you who you are." The idea we have formed of Christ—not to raise problems or to argue or debate, but only to feel his presence and love him, to seek him and find him—determines our relationship to God and our Christian relationship with man and the world. Of the utmost importance, therefore, is the response that each of us gives interiorly to the question Jesus put to those who were about to follow him: "Who do people say the Son of Man is?" (Mt. 16:14). The whole history of the Church, its whole present estate and the whole future of the kingdom, awaits the response we will give, both collectively and individually. A response which no doubt, in its countless valid formulations, serves as a basis for fraternal dialogue, for mutual enrichment, and for the fuller understanding of Christ's inner self, his Heart.

Christ is God among men, and the Son of Man before God. He is the bridge that spans all chasms and therefore He is the only mediator. He is the sacrament of God in the world and therefore he is our justification. He is the Word that comes from the Father and returns to Him, and therefore He is the key to all creation. His Incarnation and his revelation have made it possible for us to answer the question "Who do men say I am?" But it is necessary to accept and live his word about Himself if it is to grow in us, reproducing the Trinitarian love that confounds all logic: the miracle of love that

9. Center of the Christian Mystery

is a scandal to the Jews, madness to the Gentiles and a thing of no account to the unbelievers of our times.

48. It is paradoxical that we should be more disposed to accept Jesus who suffers than Jesus who loves, and that in our brothers, we make the inevitability of suffering an excuse for our egoism and our rejection of love. There is a subtle temptation to accept Jesus the man and to be reserved with Jesus the God. It is urgent that we reveal to the world precisely this Son of God made man, without watering down the mystery. To proclaim the fullness of this love whose beneficiary is all mankind, each man, the whole human race, is to give the world a point of vantage for the realization of the "*pleroma*," of the fullness of Christ in all things (Eph. 1:10).

49. Christ cannot be fully understood except in terms of his divinity; this is the essence of our faith in Him. For the free gift which He makes of Himself, there must be a corresponding freedom in man to accept Him. Both God's offering to man and the highest response of man to God coincide in Christ. I believe this is the reply we must give to modern conventionalism which speaks of "Christology from below" or ascending, and "Christology from above" or descending. Christ is the meeting point and very specifically we mean the point where the reciprocal love between God and man is consummated. Christology from below or above is a distinction which, in the profusion of current Christologies, can offer some methodological advantages. However, we must handle it with extreme care and avoid exceeding definite limits. Otherwise we will cause division in something which cannot be divided. Christ who came down from Heaven, is the same Christ who, having completed the Pascal Mystery, is at the right hand of the Father. Our knowledge and experience of his person cannot be derived only from the "Word" taken as the point of departure, nor only from the historical Jesus of Nazareth. It is dangerous to think one can theologize starting exclusively from Jesus to arrive at knowledge of Christ, or starting from Christ to arrive at a knowledge of Jesus.

50. A mention of Teilhard de Chardin is inevitable in this context. He saw Christ Jesus as the single focal point of the

universe. Of course, we need not be in agreement with each and every step of his line of reason. But I mention him here because he inspires respect as the scholar who made the most honest scientific reflection compatible with an exceptional spiritual perceptivity and responsiveness. Teilhard professed an impassioned attachment to the heart of Christ, and on two levels. One, a pure and simple devotion to the heart of Jesus along the lines of the typical presentation of this devotion at the end of the 19th and beginning of the 20th century. This he professed openly and without reserve. It is the heart of Jesus, which, in his spiritual life, is his standby in the extraordinary difficulties which he encountered in his activities as a scientist. It is the Sacred Heart of his diary, of his correspondence and of spiritual direction. The other level—and perhaps this division would irritate Teilhard—is that of Christ the "omega point" of the universe, whom he instinctively knows and who can be defined tentatively only in an act of love. Starting from the conviction that the universe is evolving and that each stage is meaningful only in terms of its relationship to the preceding stages, Teilhard concludes that the process as a whole must have a reason and an end, one omega point which is already virtually contained in the process itself and directs it from within providing its dynamism and meaning. A few months before his death in 1951 he writes in his diary a sentence which indisputably reveals the final stage of his thought: "The great secret, the great mystery: there is a heart in the world (Fact of Reflection), and this heart is the Heart of Christ (Fact of Revelation). (...) This mystery has two stages: the Center of Convergence (the Universe concentrates in one center), and the Christian Center (this center is the Heart of Christ). Perhaps I am the only man who says this. But I am convinced this expresses what each man, each Christian feels" (Journal, cahier VI, p. 106).

IV. God is Love

Heart of Christ Approach to the Trinity

51. In these pages the word love has been used deliberately more than the word charity, even though some people would reserve the word "love" for the relations within the Trinity, and would prefer

9. Center of the Christian Mystery

charity as more appropriate for fraternal love. Love has a more general connotation.

Apart from the fact that it renders better and, it seems, more scientifically the term and also the biblical concept, the analogy is diminished a little when one speaks of the affective relationships within the Trinity and those which exist among men. We start from the fact that through grace we are admitted to participation in the divine life, that is to say, to the intimacy of the Father and the Son in the Spirit. The philosophic terms that we apply to the Trinity, (nature, persons, relations) leave the mystery intact and must cede their place to the word: love. "God is love" (1 Jn. 4:16). We accept that we cannot understand the mystery though we know that through love we are included in it: the Father and Son assume us in the Spirit making us partakers of the fullness of their love. Those who have accepted the mystery of Christ, says St. John, "will live in the Son and in the Father; and what is promised to you by his own promise is eternal life" (1 Jn. 2, 24–25). This is possible in virtue of the love "that God has poured into our hearts through the Spirit which has been given us" (Rom. 5:5).

52. But love, when defined, not by its object, but by the interior disposition of the one who loves, can only be one. That is why supernatural love for one's neighbor, whom Christ loves, and whom we love for Christ's sake, is a way to draw near to the Trinity. Love of neighbor therefore, and not only of God, is a theological virtue.

Especially for those who have consecrated their lives to the service of others following the evangelical counsels which have no other foundation but love, it is a way of direct access to the intimacy of the Trinity.

Contemplatives in Action

53. Is this not what we mean by contemplatives in action? It is only a matter of an intellectual approach and intentional reference of our activities to the Lord. It is also to love Him through our works and in all things (the expression is Ignatian but the concept is authentically Pauline), especially our brothers, since both contemplation and action have for that cause and end the one God,

who is love and who commands us to love. The clarity with which we see God—and love Him—in our neighbor is the measure of our spiritual coherence. This is "the illumination of the eyes of the heart" (Eph. 1:8); this is the highest test that "God's seed remains in us and is living" (1 Jn. 3:19). This divine "seed" is nothing else but the principle of life, the Spirit who is at the same time, personification and fruit of love. We turn to man and we find God. It is the theological sublimation of our fraternal relationship.

54. Whoever lives in this light of undivided love for God and man, is not afraid to go forth into the world, because man will not be an occasion to interrupt his dialogue with God. On the contrary, they are so many more occasions for his encounter with God. Still more, in today's world characterized by unbelief, peopled by men and women who are not aware that they are the center of the love of the Trinity, or who deny it, one discovers God through the great vacuum that their ignorance or neglect has left in their hearts.

55. The love which takes us to the Trinity is the foundation and strength of our community bonds. Our community has meaning only if we live in love. It is the love Christ had and has for each of us that has brought us together. Christ loves us individually, yes, but also as a group. It is the personal response of each of us to this love of Christ and the union of all these responses put together that casually establishes our group. As long as we are and remain united by Him and for Him, He is in our midst. Our plurality reproduces the plurality of Trinitarian love, which is all self-giving participation and communion. More than the community of faith—although it is that too—it is the community of love or, if one prefers, the community of love that is born from the community of faith, that constitutes the formal element of a fraternal community. This is the deep meaning of the joyful exaltation of togetherness which Ps. 133 expresses: "How good, how delightful it is for all to live together like brothers." It is an old experience of the Christian community that is renewed in us, that of being "of one heart and one mind" (Acts 4:42). He who gives reproduces in himself the generosity of the Father; he who receives reflects the submissiveness and docility of the Son, the bond of theological love that unites us bears the mark of the Spirit.

56. All that we have said of the Trinity, of love... is full of anthropological references. Is it not possible to express ourselves in any other way? Faced with this mystery our mind are brought to a halt; the only entry is by way of the heart. And we enter into it more deeply and more vitally when our hearts are attuned to the Heart of Christ. This is, after all, what is expressed by the ancient prayer which the author of the Book of Chronicles puts on David's lips:

"Yahweh, God of our ancestors, of Abraham, of Isaac, of Israel, watch over this forever, shape the purpose of you people's heart, and direct their hearts to you" (I Chron. 29:18).

PART THREE

Pastoral Orientations

10

JESUS CHRIST IS ALL

Interview Given in 1981 and Published in 1982

This is a passage of Father Arrupe's talks with Fr. Jean Claude Dietsch, published originally in French (1982) and then in English (by the Institute of Jesuit Sources) under the title "One Jesuit's Spiritual Journey: Autobiographical Conversations with Jean-Claude Dietsch, S.J." pages 37–40. In it, Father Arrupe has sketched the origin of his own devotion to the Heart of Jesus, and what this devotion has represented in his long and rich pastoral experience, within and outside the Society.

Jean-Claude Dietsch: *Now, after such rich and meaningful reminiscing, I return to my question: For you, who is Jesus Christ?*

Pedro Arrupe: That same question was asked to me, unexpectedly, during an interview which I gave on Italian television about five years ago. The question took me by surprise, and I answered it in a completely spontaneous way: "For me Jesus Christ is everything." And today I am giving you the same answer with still more strength and clarity, "For me Jesus Christ is *everything*." So, I would define what Jesus Christ represents in my life as *"everything."*

He was and he is my ideal from the moment of my entrance into the Society. He was and he continues to be my way; he was and he still is my strength. There is no need to explain at length what that means. Take Jesus Christ from my life and everything would collapse—like a human body from which someone removed the skeleton, heart, and head.

Dietsch: *Don't you think that, even before you entered the Society, there were already some elements of this great ideal in your life?*

Arrupe: Of course, even if they were in a very embryonic form. Through the Eucharist and simple family devotions—especially devotion to the Sacred Heart—my father and mother cultivated the seed that the Society would develop later. Or better, that which the Sacred Heart himself planted, thanks to my parents, was cultivated later, thanks to the Society.

Dietsch: *The person of Jesus Christ is very complex. What aspects have impressed you the most?*

Arrupe: It is true that the person of Jesus Christ is, from one point of view, very complex or, if you will, it presents multiple aspects. But in reality, it is very simple: Whether Jesus Christ appears as a weak, fragile child or as the all-powerful; whether he is being affectionate with the little children or severe with the Pharisees, all is unified and rooted in one single aspect which is that of love; it is there that the person of Christ has a perfect unity and its greatest depth. What was for me, from the novitiate on, a simple intuition is enriched daily and has become very fruitful. And the Heart of Christ as a symbol of this love has sustained me greatly in my life and has given me the key to understand the Lord without difficulty.

Thus, this love gives life to everything else. Jesus Christ is a friend to me, especially in the Eucharist. Mass and prayer before the tabernacle nourish my thoughts and my activities. This should explain to you why I am so deeply shocked with the ideas of those few who move away from the Mass and the Blessed Sacrament, and who try to justify this attitude by their theological stance. How I would like to see St. Ignatius listening to such nonsense! What a treasure those persons lose who do not understand what the Mass is, nor what it meant to St. Ignatius and to so many other Jesuits—great theologians or simple brothers—who entered deeply into his sacramental intuitions.

We must insist without ceasing on this fundamental truth: Jesus Christ is the Incarnate Word; he is the way to the Father; and for us Jesuits he is the answer to the prayer addressed by Ignatius to Mary in the chapel at La Storta near Rome, "that she place me with her Son." Such is also my continual prayer for the Society, "that Mary place us with her Son."

10. Jesus Christ is All

Dietsch: *I am aware that the Heart of Jesus, which has such a fundamental and constant place in your life, appears only rarely in your numerous letters, allocutions, and conferences during your term as Superior General.*

Arrupe: You are right.

From the time of my novitiate, I have always been convinced that in what we call "devotion to the Heart of Jesus" is contained a symbolic expression of the Ignatian spirit and an extraordinary effectiveness both for personal perfection and for a fruitful apostolate. I still have this conviction.

Thus, it may seem strange that, during my term as General, I have spoken relatively little on this theme. But there is a reason for this which we could term pastoral, especially with regard to the Society. Faced with the emotional reactions and aversions which manifested themselves a few years ago concerning even the expression "Sacred Heart," a phenomenon which had its origin, in part, in certain exaggerations and emotional manifestations, it seemed to me that it was necessary to allow some time to pass during which that emotional reaction—which, while understandable, was hardly rational—could disappear.

I had, and I still have, the firm belief that a spirituality of so great a worth, which uses a symbol (see Eph. 1:18) so universal and human and a word, "heart," which in language is considered to be an *Urwort* ("source word" or "key word"), will fairly soon find its place once again. We will succeed little by little in revitalizing the cult of the Heart of Jesus but without imposing it with an insistence which would only serve to aggravate or reawaken the reaction of rejection which occurred in the 'fifties and 'sixties.

It might seem to us that these kinds of symbols as expressions of our faith are suited only to poorly educated or even ignorant people. The words of Jesus tell us exactly the opposite: "I bless you, Father... for hiding these things from the learned and the clever, and revealing them to mere children" (Mt. 11:25; see also Lk. 10:21). If we want to identify with the "mere children," the poor, the little ones, is this not an excellent way to imitate them and adopt their attitudes with regard to the Lord? "I assure you, unless you change and become like little children, you will not enter the kingdom of heaven" (Mt. 18:3). We could translate these words of Christ thus: "If you want, as individuals and as the Society, to enter into the treasures of the Kingdom and to help to build it up with an extraordinary efficacy, imitate the poor whom you want to serve. You say often that the poor have taught you more than books. Then learn also from them this obvious lesson: Love Jesus Christ by entering through the gate of the simple love of his Heart."

In Japan I never hesitated to consecrate, at their request, a number of very modest households to the Sacred Heart. I knew and they knew that it was one of the best ways possible to approach God, the Father of all humanity.

II

CONSECRATION OF JAPANESE FAMILIES TO THE SACRED HEART

Extracts from Fr. Arrupe's Book "I Lived the Atomic Bomb and Memories"

In his well-known book "Yo viví la Bomba Atomica y Memorias" (Published by 'Editorial Patria S.A.—' Av. Uruguay 25—Apartado Postal 784—Mexico City D.F.— Mexico), Father Arrupe gave an account of the first years of his missionary life in Japan. From it we cull a few anecdotes that reveal his personal devotion to the Heart of Jesus and the influence this exercised in his pastoral activity in Japan.

In the first days of his ministry, Father Arrupe was asked by a community of sisters in Tokyo to consecrate their house to the Sacred Heart. This consecration proved also very effective in several catholic homes. Not a few missionaries in Japan found that this practice was working wonders of grace in the Japanese soul. One day they decided to consecrate the Mission of Yamaguchi to the Heart of Jesus. This strengthened them for the ordeal which was soon to come—of imprisonment and exile of some of their group.

1. My First Apostolate in Tokyo

When I saw that I could manage the Japanese language with some ease, I decided to undertake some concrete ministry on my own. I didn't know where to make a start, when Divine Providence put me on a path which I had just to follow.

One day, the sisters of a religious community in Tokyo which I was visiting—I don't remember on what occasion—approached me.

"Father, we would like to consecrate our house to the Sacred Heart of Jesus and we cannot find a priest with the time to come."

"Don't worry, sisters; I'll come and do it." They saw heaven open before them.

"When will you do it, Father? If you wish, right now," they said.

"Let me prepare a consecration in Japanese and we shall later set a date."

In fact, after a few days, I turned up in the convent at a time pre-arranged with Mother Superior, with my act of consecration and my little exhortation of two or three pages.

It was a simple ceremony, short but with all the delicate touches with which nuns know how to enrich anything connected with the Lord's service.

That gave me an idea. As long as I was stationed in Tokyo, I could dedicate myself to consecrate families to the Sacred Heart of Jesus. Thus, without breaking new ground in some other ministry for which I did not consider my knowledge of Japanese sufficient, I could strengthen the foundations of what others had already built. Without the difficulties inherent to an untried apostolate, I would have the advantage of working in a well tested ministry.

I never regretted that step. I began with some well-known Catholic homes, and other families followed that contacted me in various ways. More than a hundred homes were soon consecrated to the Sacred Heart.

2. Marvels of Grace

None of the marvels of grace were lacking that the Lord has promised, through some of his confidants, to those who consecrate their hearts and hearths to him. How many times could I feel the grace of conversion in those brief moments of a surrender that was intended to endure. Often enough as I was treading with my bare feet the *tatamis* of the homes which I was entering for the consecration ceremony, I could see some sullen faces that betrayed resistance.

These were families in which the parents, or perhaps a widowed mother, were Catholic. But among the children of the family there was at times that division which Christ came to put on earth, even among persons bound by the closest bonds of relationship. Some of the sons and daughters were Catholic, others buddhist, shintoist or indifferent. Naturally that ceremony openly Christian, could inspire not only suspicion but repugnance to the family members who did not share the Christian faith. But when in the silence of a profound faith that wanted to surrender, we started to recite the simple and generous words of consecration, when the emotion of the Catholic members gave way to furtive tears or to unabashed weeping, the indifferent members in that microcosmic family felt that, under the natural stir of those new sentiments, grace was at work with all the supernatural thrust of what is divine.

Staunch but mistaken non-Christians, Protestants sticking out like splinters of a fractured bone in Catholic families, unbelievers who had lost faith in their deities, began to feel that the shower of God's blessings—no less real for their not knowing it—was more powerful than their obstinacy or ignorance. From passive spectators watching an inescapable scene, not a few became fervent catechumens with the certain promise of a coming baptism that would make them members of the Church.

3. A Solution for Japan

The consecration of families to the Sacred Heart of Jesus is everywhere a great thing; but it is especially so in Japan. The great problem in Japan is not only the conversion of individual persons, but equally so the keeping alive of the flame of faith lest it should be extinguished in the whirlwind of so much material progress.

A Khoikhoi convert to Christianity needs hardly to fear that his faith suffer shipwreck from reading a pornographic novel which has not been nor will ever be translated into his language. His faith will not be endangered by an atheistic philosophy that which does not ignore God but attacks him—because no book of this type will ever fall into his hands. He will not drink in the poison of a movie that brings death to his soul amidst the allurements of a placid euthanasia. A Khoikhoi convert has already one foot in heaven.

A Japanese person, in contrast, reads everything, knows everything, sees everything in the movies and TV. They are extremely curious, and since in the world there seems to be more evil than good, their spirit of a new convert, weighed down by a centuries-old tradition of paganism, is further loaded by the mire of the twentieth century which, putting God aside, has placed on the altar raised to the golden calf of the Israelites of Sinai, the idol of materialistic progress and ideologies.

A Japanese young man or young woman will more easily preserve the faith if in their home they find a counterpoise to the pagan mentality that envelops them and frequently suffocates them. Marooned in the small barren island of a faith devoid of firm autonomous roots, they have to fight a lonely battle like heroes. This happens more frequently among the intellectual class. Statistics of Catholic students who study outside the Catholic atmosphere in which they received baptism show that as many as 30% of them have abandoned the faith.

This is the reason why the consecration of the families to the Sacred Heart of Jesus has a decisive influence in the life of these youths. Faith and religion is not something to be practiced in the *Kyokai*, in church alone. It is something much more intimate which is lived also within the four walls of even the poorest home. So when, owing to work or study time tables, the doors of the mission chapels remain practically closed, only in homes consecrated to the Sacred Heart can our Catholics find the supernatural strength they need to support their faith.

To convert a Japanese in a solidly Catholic family is to gain a fervent Christian. To convert a Japanese in a family where the atmosphere is hostile is to set them on a path that will often end in heroism... and the heroes are few. To change hostility into sympathetic understanding is to switch the current of a soul, so that from a stream of doubt it may run smoothly along another of certainty that finally flows with increasing security into a haven of peace and happiness.

4. The Devotion to the Heart of Christ and the Japanese Soul

The intimate element of friendship and loving reparation contained in the devotion to the Sacred Heart penetrates easily into the soul of a Japanese neophyte. To a greater or lesser degree it would be complicated, and certainly useless at the beginning, to enter into debate and subtleties about the material and the formal object of this devotion; on whether our attention has to rest chiefly on the Heart as a symbol of Christ, or on Christ symbolized in the Heart.

A convert of yesterday has not got, except in very rare cases, the sufficient capacity to penetrate into the depths where the obscure problems of philosophy or theology are debated. But he can easily grasp other more human elements which often prove adequate for a rudimentary religious instruction. The friendship which we owe to Christ our Friend who died for us, the reparation that our sins and the sins of others demand, love as a response to the love which God bestows on us all the time—these are concepts which seem obvious to the convert and draw admirable reactions from him.

Furthermore, he finds in these values a positive effort which religion exacts from us as a complement to the more negative outlook which might seem to predominate in the Decalogue. Alongside the "no" which precedes most of the Commandments, there is the "yes," with the positive sign, with the stress on surrender that prevails in our relations with the Heart of Christ. And in this coexistence of "no" and "yes," the convert lives a Christian faith which is much more conscious and complete. For the "no" encloses an implicit desire of self-giving to Christ: therefore I give myself to you.

5. Until I Discover His Presence

I remember that at the time when I was making my first observations and reflections on this matter, I was greatly struck by the sight of a catechumen, a young girl who used to spend long hours kneeling or squatting before the Blessed Sacrament. She would enter the chapel and, walking with that silence peculiar of one who from childhood is accustomed to walk barefooted and noiselessly, she would slowly advance and get as close to the tabernacle as her respect permitted, and there she remained motionless, indifferent to all that surrounded her.

One day we met as she was leaving the chapel. We fell to talking and little by little, without forcing the conversation, I brought in the subject of her visits to the Blessed Sacrament. One of her phrases gave me the opportunity to ask her:

"What are you doing all the time before the Blessed Sacrament?" Without a moment's hesitation, as if she had prepared an answer beforehand, she replied:

"Nothing."

"What do you mean nothing?" I insisted. "How can you remain so long without doing anything?"

This sharpening of my question in order to remove all ambiguity seemed to upset her a little. This time, faced with my judicial inquiry, she was a little more slow in answering.

At last she opened her lips and said: "What do I do before the tabernacle? Well, I am there." And she was silent once more.

To a superficial mind she had said little. But in reality she had left nothing unsaid. Her few words contained the whole truth of those endless hours spent before the tabernacle. Hours with a friend, hours of intimacy in which nothing is asked, nothing is given. You just are there, together.

Unfortunately, too few can grasp the meaning of this "being with Christ," for if this "being there" is to be real, it must contain a surrender to Christ in the tabernacle, that has no other object than "to be there," without doing anything, just keeping him company—if this can be said to be doing nothing.

6. Children Discover the Sacrifice of Reparation

Another case, chronologically parallel, though of a different type, happened to me in a catechism center on the outskirts of the city. The center was attended by slum boys, some already Christian, the rest—as they say in some regions of Spain—to be Christianized. I explained to them the value of sacrifices offered to Christ with the purpose of reparation, and put up a card box,

11. Consecration of Families

pretending to be a letter box, in order that they might drop in their petitions and offerings.

One day, two of the boys who regularly attended the classes had a violent fight that ended in a complete break of diplomatic relations. Each one withdrew to a corner, and with the pout proper of angry children they did not talk to each other the whole afternoon.

"*Shimpusama,*" the other boys told me; Itsuo-san and Takeo-san had a fight."

"What happened to them?" I curiously inquired.

"*Saa,* Takeo-san is in a bad *Kimochi* (bad temper) today; he always gets angry."

Those *saa* of admiration showed me that, although things had not been serious, the quarrel had impressed all the other boys. My curiosity was aroused and I wished to see the result of that childish split, because there was a special relationship between the two boys.

Itsuo-san was 8 years old; few in number but enough for him to have been given by his parents a doctorate of sufficiency to move in the streets by himself without being accompanied. Takeo-san, a small boy of only five years, had not attained that proficiency and required someone's company whenever he had to go out of the house.

As the two boys lived in the same suburb, they had agreed that when going to school or catechism, Itsuo-san passed by the street where Takeo-san lived, and both went together; they did the same when returning. That evening they had a problem. They had quarreled, it was getting late and they had to go home. I knew the situation and was wondering how the conflict would be resolved. Most of the boys had already come to say goodbye and only a few remained talking happily—the two rivals with their sullen faces.

While I was talking with the last stragglers, I could see that the bigger boy was moving hesitantly towards little Takeo-san and was telling him something which from my observation point I could not understand. But those must have been friendly words, for Takeo gave his hand, without either of them opening their mouth to speak. They were going, though not yet in the best of terms; but they were going together, which was what mattered. For Takeo's problem was that he could not return by himself.

When all the boys had disappeared I opened the letter box with the offerings, emptied it, and before adding them to the the previous heaps to burn them all at the foot of the statue of the Sacred Heart on the last day of the novena, I noticed one, unsigned as all the rest, but with content that identified its author. I read: "For you, I made peace with Takeo-san, even though he was wrong, and not me. For you, I will accompany him home, like nothing happened."

The paper was soiled, the margin of an old envelope. But its content was of the highest spiritual value. That eight-year-old, who at home and in the public school had been taught that vengeance is a manly virtue, had mastered his burning temper to offer peace and friendship and, what his rival needed most at the moment, the help necessary to return home.

These are marvels of grace indeed and mysteries of human freedom. The culprit had no courage to overcome his pride and recognize his fault. On the other hand, Itsuo, with a delicacy of conscience that is amazing for a recently converted boy from the slums, offered that stroke of generosity to the Heart of Jesus which culminated in his own humiliation in the benefit of another.

He was just eight-years-old but he had grasped the essence of the devotion to the Sacred Heart with the thoroughness of a consummate ascetic. He knew no nice distinctions and details, but he had learned that the best test of his love of God was to be found in his own self-effacement and personal sacrifice.

7. The Promises of the Sacred Heart

Another example of the great effectiveness of the consecration to the Sacred Heart in the apostolate occurred when I contacted a Japanese lady with her son and daughter, whose husband was the only non-Catholic in the family. They were fervent Christians; he was religiously indifferent and permitted them to practice their faith, which he regarded with coldness not devoid of some contempt.

11. Consecration of Families

One day the wife came to ask me to consecrate their home to the Sacred Heart of Jesus. She wanted the Lord to reign fully in the house by drawing the believers close to him and by healing the blindness of the last member who did not have the light of truth. I agreed to do the needful. What else could I wish for? I had already consecrated a number of homes, a practice which constituted almost my first apostolic adventure in Japan.

There was, however, a hurdle to clear and a reef we had to dodge if we did not want to crash in defeat: this was the husband's strong aversion against having a religious ceremony which we might call public, performed in his own home. We had therefore a *sōdan* or meeting in which we scheduled to have the act of consecration at a time when only the mother and the two children were at home. This was not difficult. On the appointed day I presented myself at the door of the house at the exact time, armed with the formula of consecration in Japanese which I used for such occasions.

The wife came out to meet me. I expected to see in her face the joy proper of the ceremony which she had asked me to preside, but I found her very much troubled. Something had gone wrong with her calculations. "Father," she told me straightaway, "my husband is at home." That left me speechless. Our plans seemed to collapse. He would probably be opposed to having the ceremony performed. "It might be better," I told her hesitantly, "to leave it for some other day."

"No, Father," she replied; "I don't think we should put it off. For a long time I have wished to take this step, and some difficulty has always cropped up. I think we can do it quietly in another room which he is not using, without disturbing him."

"Whatever you think is best," I told her; "you have the last word." "Let us try our luck," she said; "and may God help us."

"We entered one of the rooms, We hung a picture of the Sacred Heart from the wall, and without any other solemnity or singing, we knelt before the picture, the two children, the mother and myself. We began to pray in silence. I said a few words and then, phrase by phrase, I recited the consecration, slowly so that the meaning might sink in more deeply.

We had hardly finished the recitation, when suddenly and most unexpectedly the *fusuma* or curtain that separated that room from the next was drawn and there, framed in the doorway, stood the master of the house, in an attitude which did not seem to be his usual one. When I saw him enter I remained silent, and his wife and the children were frightened wondering what the consequence of that interruption might be.

For a moment he looked at the four of us, and then suddenly, breaking down in tears like a child, he said these words to me: "I wish to be baptized." He said nothing else. He couldn't. He was deeply touched by God's grace which had been at work in him in a manner which we might call miraculous. His past resistance, his hostility, his indifference, all had vanished under the influence of the voice of the Spirit.

Here we had further proof that the Heart of Christ keeps his promise of reigning in the homes where he is enthroned. It was, moreover, a convincing example of the power of the joint prayer of a mother and children when all ask for the conversion of the father, the only stray member of the family.

8. The Missionaries Also Consecrate Themselves

In that mysterious fight for the conquest of souls, we the missionaries of Japan were constantly feeling our helplessness. In God alone could we put our trust. Therefore, with redoubled faith we consecrated to him our efforts as sowers and harvesters. We had done this individually dozens of times before but a day came when, in order to draw all the possible fruit from the rough edges of our daily life and work, we decided to do it together as a group.

Not without emotion we, all the Spanish missionaries of the area, knelt down before a statue of the Sacred Heart. There, recalling his promises of special blessings and his desire for a loving response, we poured out our petitions with absolute confidence in his goodness. In our consecration we blended the most profound theology of commitment with the most intimate sentiments of personal dedication.

On behalf of all, with a measured and serene language, Father ... read out the following words:

11. Consecration of Families

"*Consecration of the Mission of Yamaguchi to the Sacred Heart of Jesus.*

"Lord, here you have us prostrate at your feet, in the very place where Xavier, with his heart torn asunder but full of trust, bent also his knees before you.

"Lord, we wish that from today this budding Mission of Yamaguchi be in a special manner the Mission of your Heart! We therefore today from the bottom of our hearts consecrate it to you.

"Eternal King and Universal Lord! You chose what is weak in the world to shame the strong. Here you have the weakest of the missionaries trying to win this region for you, this region where Xavier labored with so much zeal. Conscious of the futility of all human means if unaided by your grace, and feeling the scant efficacy of the ordinary methods of the apostolate in this land which you wished to entrust to us, we can only trust in your promises. We blindly trust in your words, 'I will give an extraordinary efficacy to the labors of those who propagate the devotion to my Heart.' And since we need this extraordinary strength, today we promise to be true apostles of your Heart, living a life of love and reparation. Grant us, Lord, the grace that by our total self-effacement, this Mission be soon an eloquent proof of the truth of your promises.

"We, in turn, in the presence of the Divine Majesty, through the mediation of the Immaculate Virgin Mary, of the holy Patriarch St. Joseph, our Father St. Ignatius, and the first missionary of Yamaguchi, St. Francis Xavier and all the holy apostles and martyrs of Japan, promise you with your help and grace to spend our energies and our life for this ideal alone: that all the souls you have committed to our care and the entire world know the inexhaustible riches of your Heart and be consumed in your love."

And the Lord heard our prayers. He heard them—today we see with our own eyes what we then believed in faith—in ways unsearchable for our human understanding. We became victims of our limitations. His desire was that our nascent Mission should be like the mustard seed which begins to sprout. But for this, as a memorial of his Passion, he willed that his loving and redemptive Providence should be accompanied by our disappointment, sufferings and fears.

He tested our faith, as he did with Peter walking on the water. And so, before the glorious brightness of the era that is already dawning, he willed that we should go through a dark night, like his own night of the Passion, and through a complete abandonment on the part of men. Outwardly, the reply to our consecration was jail for me and exile for Father González Gil. However, what appeared to be a step backward in the field of our apostolic opportunities, was only the end of the tough period which was already opening into the beginning of a new era, easier and blessed with many more conversions—the period in which we now live.

Today we are permitted to speak of Christ without interference or unfounded suspicions. "Lord, your judgments are not our judgments, nor your ways our ways..."

12

A DEVOTION FOR OUR TIMES

Homily at the Church of the Gesù

Rome
June 1965

One month after his election as General, Father Arrupe was invited to preside over the celebration of the feast of the Sacred Heart at the Gesù. His homily reflects some of the doubts that arose during the Second Vatican Council and the 31st General Congregation still in progress at the time. It also opens new horizons lit up by his acute vision, and shows his keen sensitivity that resonates with people still today.

Some of the characteristic tendencies of people today find an answer in the person of the loving Christ. These needs and aspirations are: unity in spite of many divisive forces; the control of the technological progress that threatens humanity's destruction; the respect for each person's personality and freedom in the face of a growing oppression and violence; the yearning for peace and security in the midst of today's instability and constant fear.

The Holy Father Paul VI, the best interpreter of the wishes of our Lord, in February of this year addressed a letter to all the Bishops to remind them of the second centenary of the liturgical feast of the Sacred Heart. Here is a paragraph of this letter which shows the Pope's mind:

"It is our wish that the deep and hidden doctrinal foundations that throw light on the infinite treasures of the love of the Heart of Christ be explained to all categories of the faithful in the most suitable and complete manner."

In fact, there is today in some the tendency to disparage the cult of the Sacred Heart, or at least to consider it less opportune for our times.

But if we listen to the words of the Pope carefully, we shall see precisely that he stresses the opportuneness of this cult for the Catholics of today. Pius XII, repeating the words of the great pontiff Leo XIII, called this cult, ("a most acceptable form of piety, containing a powerful remedy for the healing of those very evils which today bring distress and disquiet, more acutely and widely than ever, to the individual and the whole human race"). Pius XII did not hesitate to state that in this devotion to the Sacred Heart are to be found "a summary of all our religion and, moreover, a guide to the most perfect life" (Encyclical *Haurietis aquas,* nn. 14–15).

1. Christ is the Center

Jesus, in St. Paul's expression, is the center of all creation (Col. I: 17–18): heaven and earth and sea, angels and men. He is the center of all and therefore all things are held together in him. But searching more closely still, we shall find that in Christ himself there is something which is "central," that brings together everything that is in him; a center toward which all the points of the circumference converge; a center from which all the lines start to the periphery. This core is his love, symbolized in his Heart.

The love of the Word for the Father is the center of his divine life, the love that brings about the incarnation. The Word becomes Jesus the Savior and takes a heart of flesh like ours. The infinite love is to be found in a small human heart; there it finds an abode, an organ of flesh, a heart full of affection and feeling.

When Paul was announcing the great synthesis of his apostolate saying, "the love of Christ overwhelms us" (2 Cor. 5:14), he was not primarily referring to the love which Paul had for Christ but rather to the love with which Christ loved Paul the love of Christ had taken possession of his heart. Thus he could say that it was not Paul who lived but Christ who lived in Paul, Christ who loved and suffered in him.

The same happens in each member of the mystical Body of Christ who lives his faith. In him lives the love of Christ who continues loving the Father and men, who continues working and sacrificing himself. The Heart of Christ is always the center of every Christian life.

2. In Order to Attain Unity

These reflections may help to convince ourselves of what the Pope says about the devotion to the Sacred Heart of Jesus as one most suitable for our times.

The world of today tends to unity. There are groups and associations of a national character, of a European, intercontinental and even world character. In his Christmas message to the world of 1964, Pope Paul VI spoke of the evil of classism, so stringent and oppressive in contemporary society. He spoke also of party spirit and factiousness which oppose ideologies, methods, interest and organizations in the very tissue of the community. On the one hand, these complex and very extensive social phenomena unite men who have common interests; but on the other hand, they create insurmountable gaps between the various categories. They convert their systematic opposition into a way of life that gives a gloomy and embittered aspect of discord and hatred to our society which is thoroughly developed from the technical and economic point of view.

All these aspirations of mankind to unite in spite of all barriers and dividing walls, because it feels itself to be one in its origin, nature and rights, are aspirations profoundly Christian. They find, however, and they will ever find insuperable obstacles, until the point is reached when all share in some manner that catalyzing element which is the love of Christ. For this love impels each one to give himself to the community in a brotherly gift, and assures that each one receive the gifts of the others. Only in the strength of the Heart of Christ is each one of us able to overcome selfishness in favor of the community.

3. To Glorify God through Science

The world of today stands in need of the Heart of Christ for its unprecedented achievements in the technological field.

The discoverers of new worlds have full right to be proud of their conquests; but they are mistaken when they try to divorce science from religion, when they separate God from the beauty of the world he has created. When science and technology take this road, they call heaven's curse upon themselves.

From whom shall we, puny men molded from dust, learn to be humble, to maintain ourselves in the truth? From the Heart of Christ. "In him are hidden all the treasures of wisdom and knowledge" (Col. 2: 3), and yet he said, "I do not seek my glory... My teaching is not mine, but his who sent me" (Jn. 7:16). Jesus, man, in whose hands "all authority in heaven and earth" (Mt. 28: 18) had been placed, made himself small before his heavenly Father and was pleased to acknowledge that all he had he had received from him.

Jesus Christ was not in need of forcing himself to live only for his Father's glory. His humility sprang from his Heart, from his love for the Father.

Following Jesus Christ along this path of love and truth, man can pursue his scientific research and glory in his technological conquest with freedom and security. Through them he will glorify his heavenly Father, and his discoveries will never turn into tools of hatred and destruction.

4. To Have an Incalculable Source of Energy

The world of today, and specially our youth, feels intoxicated with the new wine of the atomic force. They exult in the thought that in their hands they have an almost unlimited source of energy. We have therefore a reason, my dear brothers, to say that today more than ever before we need that the Heart of Jesus remain with us or return to our world. And the reason is precisely this: we live in the atomic age. It is as though an insane brat had got hold of a loaded pistol.

Journalists have tried to give prominence these days to a period of my life when Providence willed that I should foul myself in the zone blasted by the atomic bomb of Hiroshima and that I should escape unhurt.

Well then, I remember that when I was still under the terrible impression of the catastrophe, in a conversation with some young students we were commenting the power of the weapon employed, and calculated the thousands of casualties in our neighborhood and those which might be expected as a consequence. I remember how, after a pessimistic diagnosis by the youths, a spontaneous observation occurred to me which impressed them profoundly: "And after all, my dear friends, in spite of this new powerful weapon and any other that may still come, you must know that we have a power much greater than the atomic energy: we have the Heart of Christ. But while the atomic energy is destined to destroy and atomize everything, in the Heart of Christ we have an invincible weapon whose power will destroy every evil and unite the minds and hearts of the whole of mankind in one central bond, his love and the love of the Father."

5. In Order to Feel Oneself Personalized

Another characteristic feature of the modern world is the huge masses of human beings, the large and ever growing centers of population in all the continents. All are classified and categorized by electric calculators, all are filed according to their qualifications and capabilities. But meanwhile the individual is swallowed up by the crowd. Today, while triumph of personality is proclaimed, the dignity of the person is trampled underfoot, the individual is just a number to the planners, reduced to an anonymous figure, worse than a unit in the army.

In this world situation we need that Jesus Christ return to earth once more and that meeting each one of us he extend to us his hand of a friend, and calling you and me by name, tell us: "Before the world was, I knew you. I loved you in particular, and I gave my life on the cross for you." This I thought filled Paul's heart with enthusiastic wonder and made him exclaim: "He loved me and gave himself for me" (Gal. 2: 20). What more can anyone of us wish for? Even if the world forgets me, there is a God who thinks of me, knows that I exist and wishes me well!

6. In Order to Win True Freedom

People today tend to free themselves, as much as possible, from all constraining laws. They believe that independence is something sacred, the greatest of all goods. Very frequently youth want to get rid of disciplinary measures and of external regulations. The reason they give is that rules are an obstacle to the development of their own personality. Would that the interior spirit were sufficient to put a check to our inordinate tendencies! And that our passions were so mastered by reason that they no longer needed the help of external discipline!

Be that as it may, let us have recourse to the Heart of Christ in whom we shall find the secret of our full personality joined to a full interior life. We also may take as our only norm that well-known saying of St. Augustine, "Love and do as you please" (*Ama et fae quod vis*). The only condition is to have penetrated deeply into the Heart of Jesus, to love him so much that we do not think of ourselves, to love him to such an extent that we are prepared to lose everything for his sake.

7. To Remain Firm in the Midst of the Storm

Finally, another wound that afflicts the world today is instability. If we look around we shall see that everything is in a fluid state. In Europe and outside Europe, in the East and in the West, instability is the bane of many governments and political parties, fluctuation is the law in the money exchange and in the market. Changeable is the rhythm of demand and supply.

But that is not all. The world today is afraid of the instability of its own ideas and beliefs. Many people who are at the helm of human activities and trends feel uncertain about the validity of principles, rights and duties, particularly in the field of social justice. Even the philosophical structure of thought is tottering and becomes skeptical and agnostic. Repercussions of this instability are felt in the Catholic faith as well where one can perceive much vacillation and uncertainty even in private and professional life. Some would like to do away with the rigidity of dogmas...

Isn't this a sign that we need Jesus more than at any time in the past? Only he stands firm, indestructible upon the rock, while everything around him wavers in constant restlessness. Our Savior has ever remained constant in his statements of Yes or No. Through Peter he continues today to impart a feeling of security to the poor human mind, a fragile little boat tossed in the stormy ocean. We must give our minds a sure criterion. We need a source of knowledge which is ever fresh and young, today and tomorrow as it was in the days of St. Paul—the science of the love of Christ.

Paul wanted to communicate to his Christians a re-assuring certitude that will never lose sight of the love of Jesus for us. Some of the faithful in the church of Ephesus were attracted to some strange ideas and mysterious concepts. Paul tells them forcefully that there is one knowledge that transcends all others—the knowledge of the love of Christ, on which the stability of human thought depends (Eph. 5: 18).

This is a love without bounds, because the love of the Heart of Christ is infinite in depth, in its height and breadth; there are no boundaries of time or place, or limitation of persons.

This is, my dear brothers, where I invite you to fix your minds and especially your hearts; in the love of Christ we shall find stability in life, the happiness of feeling ourselves loved, security on the way. These blessings will surely be ours if in following Jesus we are led by her, who is the Mother of the eternal Wisdom, the Daughter of Love and the Lady of the Way.

13

A RESPONSE OF FAITH AND LOVE

Homily Delivered in Rome
1973

With an abundance of biblical reminiscences Father Arrupe invites his listeners, and now his readers, to make a suitable response to the "sign of love" offered by Jesus Christ on the cross with effective love for the brethren, as the most authentic expression of the genuine devotion to the Heart of Christ.

The sign of Christ on the cross is one that evokes different reactions in different people—a sign of contradiction. Some "loved darkness rather than light," and were hardened in their unbelief. Others, however, believed and their faith impelled them to love God and their neighbor.

1. The Sign of Christ Crucified

In the book of Numbers the inspired writer tells us that the Lord punished the Israelites with several plagues. One of the most terrible was the plague of serpents. Very many died of their bite. Moses pleaded for the people, and at the Lord's bidding he made a bronze serpent, set it up on a pole, "and if a serpent bit any man, he would look at the bronze serpent and live" (Num. 21: 9).

In his conversation with Nicodemus Jesus made use of this passage of the Bible as a term of comparison: "As Moses lifted up the serpent in the wilderness, so must the Son of man be lifted up, that whosoever believes in him may have eternal life. For God so loved the world that he gave his only Son, that whoever believes in him should not perish but have eternal life" (Jn. 3: 14–15). And later on, a few days before the Passover on which he was going to be crucified, Jesus said to the crowd around him: "And I, when I am lifted up from the earth, will draw all men to myself" (Jn. 12: 32).

This is that "sign of salvation" of which the book of Wisdom speaks (Wis. 16: 6). "For he who turned towards it was saved, not by what he saw, but by thee, the Savior of all" (v. 7). And the sacred book continues: "And by this thou didst convince our enemies that it is thou who deliverest from every evil. (v. 8); "thy mercy came to their help and healed them (v. 10) ... For thou hast power over life and death" (v. 13).

More explicit still is the prophet Zechariah: "They will look at him whom they have pierced" (Zech. 12: 10). Here is an invitation to look on the one who has been "transfixed," "the only begotten son," whose open side—Saint John tells us—is like a fountain of salvation: "one of the soldiers pierced his side with a spear, and at once there came out blood and water" (Jn. 19:34).

The figure of the Crucified over the earth, with his side wide open, has its roots in the Old Testament and is a compendium, as it were, of the theology of John's Gospel. It could be said that it is a summary of the whole of Christianity. More than any other symbol, this is a sign in St. John of the redeeming fecundity of the death of Christ. The open side, from which blood and water gush forth, responds to a Semitic symbolism: the wound, a sign of death (the slain lamb); and the blood and water, a sign of life and fecundity. Thus the pierced heart is the symbol of the Paschal Lamb of the New Covenant. This is the teaching of the encyclical *"Haurietis aquas"*:

"The words of the prophet Zechariah, 'they shall look on him whom they have pierced,' referred to by John the Evangelist to Jesus nailed to the cross, have been spoken to Christians in all ages (AAS xxxviii [1956] p. 339). Nothing, therefore, prevents our adoring the Sacred Heart of Jesus Christ as having a part in and being the natural and expressive symbol of the abiding love with which the divine Redeemer is still on fire for mankind" (ibid. p. 336).

Placed before Christ Crucified in deep contemplation and looking at "him whom they have pierced," from whose open side blood and water flow, we shall hear him say to us what he said to the Jews on the feast of the Tabernacles: "Standing up he proclaimed: If anyone thirst, let him come to me and drink. He who believes in me, as the scripture has said, 'out of his heart shall flow rivers of living water'" (Jn. 7:3; 7–38).

Such language was perfectly clear to Christ's audience, who saw in this "living water" the water they drew from their wells to offer it to the Lord with the fruits of the earth. These words are still more clear to us who are conscious of the drought of our souls and feel the thirst of the spirit: "My soul is thirsting for my God, the living God" (Ps. 41: 3). And with the Psalmist, our dry hearts cry to the Lord, "My soul thirsts for thee like a parched land" (Ps. 142: 6).

2. The Response of Unbelief

Many do not heed the invitation of Jesus, "If any one thirst let him come to me." Millions of human beings are distracted in the midst of life with their successes and failures, their joys and sorrows. Although in the bottom of their hearts they feel a burning thirst for perfection and happiness, they never raise their eyes to the "pierced" one, and consequently never come to know what true happiness is.

History repeats itself, and men today, as in the times of Jesus, "though they had seen so many signs before them, yet they did not believe in him" (Jn. 12: 37). They do not believe in him, nor do they accept his words: "the light shines in the darkness and the darkness has not overcome it" (Jn. 1: 5). They also refuse to accept the testimony of his works, "The world was made by him, yet the world knew, him not" (Jn. 1: 10). Nor do they accept his person. "He came to his own home, and his own people received him not" (Jn. 1: 11).

Men find Christ's language difficult to accept when he announces to them the mystery of the Eucharist (Jn. 6: 10). If they seek him, they do it out of self-interest: "You seek me, not because you saw signs, but because you ate your fill of the loaves" (Jn. 6: 26). They will come to the point of stoning him: "The Jews took up stones again to stone him" (Jn. 10: 31), and even of putting him to death (Jn. 12: 23). How appropriately John's Gospel has been called "the Gospel of the unrecognized love" (Mollat). How true it is that "men loved darkness rather than light" (Jn. 3: 19).

Here are to be found the roots of the problem of unbelief, atheism and modern secularization. The world refuses to look up to the Crucified; they are afraid of that figure, they do not know that there the fountain of living water is to be found, which will slake their thirst.

3. The Response of Faith

"Whoever thirsts, let him come and drink," says Jesus. To believe in him one must first go to him. There is no one who finds him and is not fascinated by his personality.

This happened to Nathanael on first meeting Jesus: "Rabbi, you are the Son of God! You are the King of Israel" (Jn. I: 49). The same was the case with the people of the town of Sichem who told the Samaritan woman: "It is no longer because of your words that we believe, for we have heard for ourselves and we know that this is indeed the Savior of the world" (Jn. 4: 42). And we have the great confession of the apostle Thomas: "My Lord and my God" (Jn. 20: 28). We have besides the testimony of many others: "And many came to him, and they said, 'Everything that John said about this man is true.' And many believed in him there" (Jn. 10: 41–42).

With faith comes a living in keeping with that faith. In the second letter of John we read: "I rejoiced greatly to find some of your children following the truth, just as we have been commanded by the Father" (2 Jn. 4). Life in Christ is a life whose principal purpose is love: "Whoever confesses that Jesus is the Son of God, God abides in him and he in God. So we know and believe the love God has for us. God is love and he who abides in love abides in God and God abides in him" (1 Jn. 4: 15–16).

This love, evidently, is not a mere intellectual concept; it consists in embracing the truth wholeheartedly and being penetrated by it. Without this love deep down in one's life, one cannot possess the true knowledge of God: "He who does not love does not know God, for God is love" (1 Jn. 4: 8). Genuine faith, therefore or the coming to Jesus necessarily includes the love of the neighbor: "This is his commandment, that we should believe in the name of his Son Jesus Christ and love one another, just as he commanded us" (1 Jn. 3: 23).

This is the central thought of the ethical and moral doctrine of the Evangelist John. The faith by which we believe in the "pierced Heart," would be illusory and of no avail if it did not impel us to brotherly love, for "he who does not love has not known God." It is worth noting how John proposes the love of the brethren as the true response to the love God has for us. It is clear that the love of Jesus is in the background in all the writings of John and that the Evangelist's personal love for the Lord can be felt throughout; but it is a fact that nowhere does this love of God appear expressly as a commandment or is even mentioned. On the other hand, the love of the brethren is constantly insisted upon: "Beloved, if God so loved us, we also ought to love one another" (1 Jn. 4: 11).

Saint John reduces Christianity to its greatest simplicity: believe and love. "The believer," Spicq would say, "is the one who knows what love is, and gives himself to it unreservedly" *(Agape dans el Nouveau Testament,* I, 313).

4. The Devotion to the Heart of Christ

In summary, here we have also, in its simplest and profoundest form, the essence of the true devotion to the Sacred Heart. Looking at this "book written within and on the back" (Rev. 5: 1), we can learn "the mystery of Christ in whom are hid all the treasures of wisdom and knowledge" (Col. 2:3). Gazing and reading in the Crucified Christ, with the open side, we shall recognize the Son of God "who humbled himself and became obedient unto death, even death on a cross" (Phil. 2:8). And going to him, we shall believe with a faith which, if it is genuine, will drive us to action, to the love of God which will unfailingly manifest itself in the love of our fellow men.

If God's love for us reached the point of giving us his only-begotten Son, our response to this love ought to be an absolute surrender to Christ and to the brethren. "Therefore be imitators of God, as beloved children, and walk in love as Christ loved us and gave himself for us, a fragrant offering and sacrifice to God" (Eph.

5: 1–2). Thus Pius XII could write that the cult of the Sacred Heart "contains a summary of all religion and the most perfect kind of life" (AAS xxxvi, 1944, p. 220).

This life of love for Christ and for our fellow men, which is the most perfect expression of Christian living, carries with it all the characteristics proper of the Spirit of God:

—it puts fear to flight: "There is no fear in love, but perfect love casts out fear... he who fears is not perfected in love" (1 Jn. 4: 18);

—it drives out all anguish and anxiety: "I am writing this to you that you may not sin; but if any one does sin, we have an advocate with the Father, Jesus Christ the righteous" (1 Jn. 2:11);

—it increases our confidence: "And now, little children, abide in him, so that when he appears we may have confidence and not shrink from him in shame at his coming" (1 Jn. 2:28); "In this is love perfected with us, that we may have confidence for the day of judgment" (1 Jn. 4: 17)

—it is an expression and gift of peace: "Peace I leave with you; my peace I give to you. Let not your hearts be troubled, neither let them be afraid" (Jn. 14:27);

—it is a token of victory: "Whatever is born of God overcomes the world; and this is the victory that overcomes the world, our faith" (1 Jn 5:4).

14

A FEAST OF SORROW OR JOY?

Homily Delivered in Rome

Feast of the Sacred Heart
June, 1975

This homily, preached on the feast of the Sacred Heart of the Holy Year 1975, resounds with the echoes of the Apostolic Exhortation of Pope Paul VI, published one month before, on "Christian Joy" ('Gaudete in Domino,' dated May 9, 1975, is in AAS, LXVIII, pp. 322–289). It contains an implicit answer to certain aspects, tinged with mournful tendencies, of a false devotion to the Sacred Heart.

In the depths of the person of Christ is to be found the source of his inexpressible joy, which consists in the knowledge that the Father loves him, that he is the beloved Son with whom the Father is well pleased.

The joy of Christ is the cause of the joy of a Christian. Christ's disciple should live the joy of life to the full, the joy of having been chosen, of being instruments in God's hands, of being the heirs of never ending happiness. This inner joy will foster in us a positive attitude in face of pain and suffering, the unavoidable prerequisites for the dawn of a glorious resurrection.

Today is the feast of the Sacred Heart. This is a feast that has a note of sorrow, of sadness, with the cross on the background. The side of Christ crucified appears wounded by a spear; from his pierced heart gushes blood and water. The symbol of the cross is surmounted with a crown of thorns. There is the invitation to make reparation for sins and the infidelity of men to Christ's infinite love.

All this gives to the feast of the Sacred Heart of Jesus a touch of guilt, of pain and suffering. However, in its deeper significance, this is a celebration of love, and love stands for joy and gladness and happiness.

1. A Feast Joyful and Sorrowful

Someone will say: Right, but in the case of Jesus love supposes the cross. Yet, the flames that rise from the Heart of Jesus are flames of love, and of an infinite love. And on this love rests the true meaning of the feast of the Heart of Jesus. Only in this love is it possible to grasp the mystery of redemption, just as only in this infinite love of God can we find the key to the paschal mystery. This mystery supposes the cross, but contains also the resurrection and the final glorification. Thus as Pope Paul VI put it in one of his exhortations, "The Easter proclamation *"Exulte"* sings of a mystery accomplished far beyond the expectations of the prophets of old. In the joyful announcement of Christ's Resurrection the very weakness of man is transformed, while the fullness of exultation bursts forth from the victory of the crucified Christ, from his wounded Heart, from his glorified body" (Paul VI: Apostolic Exhortation "Rejoice in the Lord," III).

We too, in reconciling this antinomy of cross and resurrection, of passion and glory, which is the mystery of Christ, must try to penetrate into the depths of his person. In him we discover an ineffable joy, a joy which is his own secret, something all his own. Jesus is happy because he knows that his Father loves him. The voice coming down from heaven at the moment of his baptism at the Jordan—"Thou art my beloved Son; with thee I am well pleased (Lk. 3: 22)—is only an external expression of the profound and continuing internal experience which Jesus had of his Father from the moment of his conception: "The Father knows me and I know the Father" (Jn. 10: 15). This mutual knowledge takes place in a complete and incessant interchange of the trinitarian love: "all mine are thine, and thine are mine" (Jn. 17: 10). In this communication of love, which is the very existence of the Son and the secret of his trinitarian life, the Father gives himself constantly and unreservedly to the Son, and the Son gives himself with an infinite love to the Father, in the Holy Spirit.

2. The Joy of Jesus Christ

The profound motive of Christ's joy will also be the motive of our true joy. This joy rests on our sharing in the divine life through the Spirit present in our innermost being; it rests on our sharing in the love with which the Father loves the Son, to which we are also called: "I made known to them thy name, and I shall make it known, that the love with which thou hast loved me may be in them, and I in them" (Jn. 17: 26).

Within the framework of this interior experience we can better understand the true meaning of the beatitude, "Blessed are you that weep now, for you shall laugh" (Lk. 6: 21); also the meaning of joy in persecution, as expressed in the other beatitude: "Blessed are you when men revile you and persecute you and utter all kinds of evil against you falsely on my account. Rejoice and be glad, for your reward is great in heaven; for so men persecuted the prophets who were sent before you" (Mt. 5: 11–12).

The Heart of Christ is the symbol of the infinite love, the love human and trinitarian, which he gives through the Holy Spirit that dwells in us. A fruit of this Spirit is joy, which has the power of transforming everything into a spiritual joy (Rom. 14: 17; Gal. 5: 22); a joy which no one can take away from the disciples of Jesus once they have come into possession of it (Jn. 13: 3; cf. 2 Cor. 1:4; 7: 4–6).

After trying to understand the joy of Christ, so intimate and profound, we can see how the spiritual gifts of knowledge, intelligence and wisdom, communicated to us by the Holy Spirit, produce as a fruit a joy that embraces our entire being. This makes us feel an intimate happiness already in this world in the midst of all tribulations, as a presage of the perfect happiness, which is to be ours forever, of the kingdom of heaven.

3. The Cause of Our Joy

This intimate joy, when experienced in all its depth and extent, is manifested in *the joy of being*. Such is the experience lived in the light of faith in him "in whom we live and move and have our being" (Acts 17: 28). It is the joy of feeling ourselves penetrated by God who gives us life, who dwells in us in the Trinity of persons, who keeps creating us at every moment, thus giving us an irrefutable proof of his infinite love.

This joy is shown also in *the joy of having been elected* "before the foundation of the world" (Eph. 1: 4) with a love of predilection, implied in this choice, for a privileged vocation "that we may be holy before him." It is the consciousness of having been the object of a divine preference: "You did not choose me, but I chose you" (Jn. 15: 16); "you are my friends." It is chiefly the awareness, confirmed by the testimony of the Spirit, that "we are children of God, and if children, then heirs, heirs of God and fellow heirs with Christ" (Rom. 8: 16–17).

This joy is *a sure joy,* well grounded on the love of Almighty God. "If God is for us, who is against us?" (Rom. 8: 31). "Who shall separate us from the love of Christ?" knowing, as we do, that even if a woman forget her sucking child, "I shall not forget you" (Is. 49: 15).

This is *the joy of one who knows that he possesses the whole deposit of faith,* the treasures of God's knowledge and wisdom, for the sake of which it is worthwhile to sell everything else in order to buy the pearl of great value. This pearl is mine!

This again is *the joy of being an instrument in the hands of God.* All that is mine is at the same time a work and a gift of God, as a result of his continuous concurrence and help, both in the natural and in the supernatural order. What a joy to be God's collaborators, his ministers and instruments, even in the highest work of infinite love, which is the salvation of the world!

Finally, there is *the joy of having been created for an eternity of bliss,* called to an eschatological vocation, destined for a life which will know no end. There our hearts tend with all the expectancy and nostalgia of one who is going home, where we shall participate "in the rejoicing of the marriage of the Lamb" (Rev. 19: 7–9). Our earthly life, with all its vicissitudes, has an eternal transcendence. We know for certain that our names are written in heaven (Lk. 10:

20), that at the end of our days a perfect and everlasting happiness is waiting for us with God, because "God will wipe away every tear from our eyes" (Rev. 7: 17).

4. In Order to Overcome Our Difficulties

It is no easy matter to understand what this joy is, in the midst "of the great tribulation" of this world (Rev. 7: 14). Faith is the only beacon that can guide our way, a living faith that may sharpen our capacity of penetration, and permit us to discern at every moment this transcendent eschatological relation. The only power capable to bend this hard rod of tribulation and suffering is the burning flame of the love of Christ. Hence in the Heart of Christ we have the symbol and the key of this divine alchemy, which transforms suffering into joy, and pain into bliss.

One thing is certain—the true joy of Christ springs from love, and the way to reach it is the way of the cross. This is a doctrine difficult to understand. The apostles themselves, in spite of the years they spent in the school of Jesus, came to understand it only little by little. The words with which Jesus upbraided the two disciples on the road to Emmaus, we could apply to ourselves: "O foolish men, and slow of heart to believe all that the prophets have spoken! Was it not necessary that the Christ should suffer these things and enter into his glory?" (Lk. 24: 25–26). But once they grasped this, the apostles were possessed of a joy which was irresistible and highly communicative (Acts 2: 4, 11). Their joy was so great that "they left the council, rejoicing that they were counted worthy to suffer dishonor for the name of Jesus" (Acts 5: 4; cf. 4:12).

Those who possess a living faith feel in themselves a plenitude of joy (Jn. 17: 13), as the first Christians did, who lived a simple life "with glad and generous hearts" (Acts 2: 46). They communicate this joy to others with their words and example, as Philip the deacon did, who in a Samaritan town "proclaimed them the Christ ... and there was much joy in that city" (Acts 8: 5–8). Paul and his companion Silas, who had been cast into prison and had their feet fastened in the stocks, passed the night "praying and singing hymns to God, and the prisoners were listening to them" (Acts 16: 23–25).

5. The Mystery of This Feast

This may help us to understand the deep meaning of the mystery of the feast of the Sacred Heart, which is a feast of love and not, as I said, one of pain and sorrow. In fact, this pain and this sorrow, a result of our lack of response to the love of Christ, is transformed, through this love, into real happiness and joy. One can then understand how Paul could describe Christ's servants "as sorrowful, yet always rejoicing" (2 Cor. 6: 10), and as "overjoyed in the midst of their afflictions" (cf. 2 Cor. 7: 4). And to the Colossians he would say, "I rejoice in my sufferings for your sake" (Col. 1: 24), inviting them to share his immense joy with him.

These thoughts may help us to take a positive attitude when faced with suffering and the cross and to expand our joy in the measure in which we share in the sufferings and the cross of Christ. "Friends, do not be surprised at the fiery ordeal which comes upon you to prove you, as though something strange were happening to you. Rather rejoice in so far as you share Christ's sufferings, that you may also rejoice and be glad when his glory is revealed" (1 Pet .4: 12–13). Or, as the apostle James writes to his disciples: "Count it a joy, my brethren, when you meet various trials" (Jam. 1:2). The key to the understanding of this mystery is the point of view which Jesus, our pioneer and perfecter of our faith, took of suffering and the cross: "For the joy that was set before him, he endured the cross despising the shame" (Heb. 12: 2).

Before concluding I would like to quote the words of Pope Paul VI in a recent document: "In the course of this Holy Year of Jubilee, 1975, we have endeavored to follow with all fidelity the promptings of the Holy Spirit, by inviting the faithful to return to the sources of joy" (*Gaudete in Domino*). The world is clamoring for joy; there is so much suffering everywhere, so much anguish, so much insecurity. The spring of joy is to be found in the Heart of Christ, symbol of the infinite love of God, who "so loved the world, that he gave his only Son" (Jn. 3: 16). This love is the fountain of our happiness, the secret that will transform all into joy, the true joy that than can fill man's heart.

Those who possess this love in all its depth and transforming power will feel it as a "living flame of love," as "a soft hand," as

14. Sorrow or Joy

"a delicate touch" that "savors of eternal life" and "in slaying thou hast changed death into life" (St. John of the Cross, vol. III, p. 40: in Allison Peers' translation of *The Living Flame of Love*, Stanza 2). Here lies the secret of human happiness, hidden to the wise and understanding, and discovered only by the simple and little ones.

My wish and prayer to the Lord is that the feast of the Sacred Heart of this Holy Year may teach us to sing in our hearts, in fullness of joy, the song of joy which is never to end. Suffering and the cross will one day be a thing of the past, but the joy of the heavenly "Alleluia" which the blessed sing already in heaven, will never come to an end.

15

WHAT CAN WE DO TO PRESENT THE DEVOTION TO THE SACRED HEART IN THE CLIMATE OF TODAY?

Some Reflections in 1975

In 1975 Father Arrupe accepted an invitation to be one of the speakers who were to address, each for about ten minutes, an audience of clergy, religious, and laity who were zealous to promote the devotion to the Heart of Christ. While preparing for this address, Father Arrupe took this occasion to reflect deeply, extensively and in writing—on how this devotion might be presented effectively amid the conflicting mentalities of that time—attitudes with which he, like Pope Paul VI, was coming into much contact. In his address he spoke without notes and used only a very small portion of what he had previously written. But the notes of his lengthier reflection were preserved, and are made public here now.

Introduction

This is a matter of such great importance that we ought to reflect in depth about the concrete procedure and the best means we can excogitate to achieve our goal: effective presentation of devotion to the Sacred Heart in the human climate of today. Otherwise, even with the best of intentions, we shall run the risk of falling into a subjective and one-sided view, an outlook characteristic of a thought-current which is too uniform and rigid. The result would be to turn our investigation and the means we use into a blind alley; or at least, we would reach a procedure far less productive, one which would lead to an end somewhat different from the one we truly seek.

In my opinion, our aim should be to explore deeply into the essence and value of devotion to our Savior's Heart, to think out how this cult can be spread as effectively and extensively as possible, and how the reign of Christ's love, symbolized by his Heart, can be established and consolidated throughout the whole world.

I. Toward Clear Formulation of Our Aim

We have no thought of calling into doubt the foundations and values of this devotion, which are based on divine revelation and the faith.

Neither are we thinking that our own present manner of conceiving the devotion is the best, or that best adapted to today's world.

We have no thought, either, of attempting to convince others by imposing our ideas on them, or of condemning those who think or express themselves differently from ourselves, insofar as they accept or reject some accidental features different from those to which we hold.

We ought to avoid locking ourselves into our own way of thinking, or judging the intentions of those who think or act in a manner different from our own.

Even less ought we to accept unconditionally, and without previous discernment, the present-day world's manner of thinking or speaking about this topic.

In contrast to all the above, we ought to recognize that a real change has occurred in theological thought; that in many matters genuine progress has been made; and that this change is irreversible, insofar as we cannot go back to what was the case in former days.

We ought, rather, to aim at discerning the present gains and assimilating them; and this presupposes our recognition of the progress made and our openness to the men and women of today.

We ought, too, to foster an attitude of humility in ourselves, to question our own selves while admitting that we can be in error, and to discern and evaluate the positions we take.

15. How to present this Devotion

We should deeply study the mentality, attitudes, and scale of values which modern men and women have, and especially those of the youths who are the basis and hope of the future, that we may learn how to adapt our own way of thinking and speaking, and how to act with greater efficacy in our apostolic work.

We should enter into a sincere dialogue with the modern world—its theologians, sociologists, pastoral ministers, youths, the Christian people in its totality.

We must be *patient;* for this fecund adaptation requires time, both for the studies in depth to be made and for the positive results to be achieved in the midst of a change so extensive in nature as this.

We must be objective in regard to accepting the results of such a study, even if those results turn out to be other than those we expected, or even perhaps contrary to our manner of thinking.

We ought to maintain the flexibility necessary to adapt our own mentality to the mentality or mentalities of today, in the midst of that orthodox and rich pluralism characteristic of modern society.

We should cultivate openness and scientific sincerity in seeking collaboration from persons who think in their own distinctive way or represent currents of theological thought different from our own.

We ought to engage in constructive labor and contact with the diverse forces operating in the Church; and likewise to avoid positions or expressions which are too rigid, and which can stir up an impression of intolerance and thereby provoke a rigid reaction. This could go so far as to cause those who think otherwise than we to withdraw into themselves and reject further dialogue as impossible. Through that we could lose the collaboration and other elements of great worth.

II. Toward Clear Formulation of Our Strategy or Manner of Proceeding

St. Ignatius states that to bring men to Christ, a wise procedure is "to enter with the interests of others in order to come out later on with our own."[1] In other words, it is wise to understand others' viewpoints and interests, that thus we may lead them more efficaciously to what is good.

To cast our gaze into another area, a principle of "marketing" is that we should understand well the circumstances of the marketplace before we try to sell our merchandise in it. To investigate and know what the demand may be is altogether necessary for success in sales.

To succeed in "selling our merchandise," the devotion to the Heart of Christ, we must know what the present condition of the marketplace is—the world of men and women whom we are addressing—in such a way that we show them our merchandise "by entering through their interests." For this, three steps will be necessary.

Step 1. **We must know what the devotion to the Sacred Heart truly is, and all that it contains.** This is the most important factor. It will require study truly profound which is theological, biblical, sociological, and the like—a study which brings us to profit from modern investigations, and through this to penetrate and understand the significance of this devotion. Such a study cannot be achieved unless much time is dedicated to it, and unless the effort is scientifically beyond reproach, multidisciplinary, objective, and carried out without setting up offensive categories of theological thought—currents.

Step 2. **We must understand the present situation of the world and of the men and women in it.** We can succeed only through a profound study of our present culture, and of its diverse ideological and sociological movements insofar as they have any bearing on our topic.

Similarly indispensable is a profound analysis of the values and scale of values current among persons of today, along with the diverse aspects which these values have in various subcultures. It entails analysis of the use of modern symbols and of the graphic representation of ideas and realities.

---

1 In *Obras completas de san Ignacio* (Madrid, 1982), Letter to Broet, pp. 678–679; see also p. 807, and *Spiritual Exercises*, [332].

Step 3. **We must explore the methods by which we can communicate and express the content of this devotion in our present cultural climate.**

In view of the modern mentality and attitudes, and of the changes already known which have created our "image culture" with all its consequences, we must reflect about the methods by which we can most effectively present and spread the spirit and total content of this devotion to precisely this concrete public. It is composed of persons very diverse who have, each one, his or her own personal history and psychology. Immediately we find ourselves in the problem of pastoral care, and that of evangelization which is both personal and collective.

We cannot rescind from any one of these three steps just listed. To achieve the third step efficaciously, the first two are necessary as means. Our end (*primum in intentione*) is precisely the communication of this devotion; but this presupposes our study of what this devotion truly is, and of the world to whom we desire to communicate it. Clearly, therefore, this effective communication will be our last step (*ultimum in executione*), something to be fully achieved only after enough time has elapsed for the first two (see *Constitutions of the Society of Jesus*, [135]).

However, this does not in any way mean that we can do nothing until the first two steps have been completely accomplished. Rather, what it does state is that to achieve the third step in a manner truly efficacious, we must be willing to wait in patience until the study required in steps 1 and 2 have advanced a goodly distance.

Hence arises the importance of starting to work soon, and in a way carefully planned, on the first two steps, which are so fundamental that without them the third cannot be accomplished. These first two steps are the most difficult, and they must be undertaken in a profound and systematic way so that they provide a firm basis for efficacious procedure.

For that, a good plan is necessary, and persons to carry it through. That is, it requires qualified personnel and sufficient economic means, two factors which are hard to find. Here, in my humble view, is the best and most difficult service which any group might furnish.

Yet only thus can we achieve full success in presenting the devotion to the Sacred Heart as a response to the human problems of today, as a firm foundation for the men or women of today who, whether believers or non-believers, are searching in anxiety for a solution to their personal and social problems.

APPENDIX

Here I suggest some topics which can well be studied. This list ought to be completed logically and amplified.

1. The great problem of men and women of today: the meaning of life.

2. The person of Christ as the object of love both religious and human from the men and women of today.

3. The person of Christ in the world of today: the acceptation (total or partial) which various groups manifest toward him.

4. The Eucharist as the present manifestation of Christ's love towards the people of today.

5. The Eucharist as something truly present among us, and the modern attitudes toward it.

6. Christ's cross as a manifestation of his love, and its meaning for persons of our time.

7. The religious spirit of our modern people.

8. Atheism, its manifestations, and its causes with their relation to present-day Christology.

9. Symbols in our culture of today: the reasons for their transformations, and the present situation in regard to the heart as a symbol.

10. The diverse expressions of genuine human love in today's world.

11. The mutual relation between a symbol and the thing signified.

12. The social dimension of Christ's love.

13. The relations between faith, charity, and justice: justice as an integrating part of the "service of faith" *(diakonia fidei)*.

14. Justice and devotion to the Sacred Heart.

Pedro Arrupe, S.J.

16

MYSTERY OF THE MERCIFUL LOVE

Homily Delivered in Rome
1979

Foreshadowing the great encyclical of John Paul II, "Dives in misericordia" but grounded on other texts of the same Pope that foreboded it, Father Arrupe presents in this homily the Heart of Jesus as the supreme revelation of the Mystery of God and of man. The history of God's love and mercy has one form and one name—Jesus Christ.

The root word "heart" has been appropriately chosen by Scripture, psychology, folklore and common sense throughout the centuries to denote the very core of the human reality and the symbolic representation of God's loving manifestation of himself and of his merciful outpouring to rebellious mankind.

1. Meaning of the Word "Heart"

In human language there are words considered to be fundamental, original, "source words," in contrast to other words known as "technical" or "useful." The former contain an enormous evocative power. They are like sea shells that collect in their innermost coils all the distant murmurs of the ocean. The other type of words are coined by man for practical and utilitarian purposes. The source words come down the ages loaded with a weight of deep persuasive connotation, evoke deep and varied ideas and sentiments, and in many cases have different meanings depending on the personal experiences of the speaker or the listener. The "technical" words are plain, concrete, applied to ideas or objects of our daily life and do not transcend tangible realities.

The word "heart" is one of those source words, fundamental, original, than go to the root of things.

"Heart" is one of these complex concepts, whether studied in biblical theology, in the popular language, or in daily life. It may be said that it expresses man in his totality and is logically anterior to the philosophical distinction between the biological body and the incorporeal spirit. "Heart" is a real symbol used to express the most original center of the psychological unity of the person, the innermost core of every human being, in which the openness to God and to other men is essentially realized.

The heart is, we might say, the consciousness of the birth of all human decisions. It is the "I" of man, his inner self, his hidden personality, in contrast to the external appearance of man. The heart is God's point of insertion into man; here is where the natural law is imprinted and the Holy Spirit infused; this is the abode of the Trinity. This is the intimate point of contact *"toto ictu cordis"* of the actasis of St. Augustine and his mother St. Monica at Ostia *(Confessions* IX, 10, nn. 23–25). For a Christian the heart represents the fountain of all his personal life, where thought, love and sentiments converge into one: *Cor meum,* says St. Augustine, *ubi sum, quicumque sum:* "My heart, where I am, whatever I am" (Conf. X, 3–4).

2. The Heart of Christ Reveals the Mystery of God

The Heart of Christ has for us a still deeper meaning. The faith experience makes it for us the infinite love of the Redeemer for the Father and for us men.

Thus the "Heart of Christ" is the indicator, so to say, pointing to us where we shall find the most profound depths of our faith. It is like a large door that opens wide to admit us to a better understanding of the depths of the one and triune God and his activity *"ad extra"* in the gift of himself. As we draw near to this divine love, symbolized by the Heart of Jesus, we shall find the most efficacious inspiration for our life of children of God and the deepest insight into so many fundamental human aspirations.

The Heart of Jesus is an open door to the secret recesses of God. Having the only-begotten Son of God as a guide we can approach, with the profoundest awe, the "Holy, Almighty, Immortal God," who has deigned "to reveal to us his mystery, which was kept secret from long ages but is now disclosed" (Rom. 16: 25–26).

Though St. John of the Cross rightly says that "the closer the soul approaches God, the blacker is the obscurity she feels through its weakness" (*The Dark Night of the Soul*, II, 16, 11: Allison Peers, p. 453); yet in this very obscurity a light emerges that allows us, in a wonderful manner, to penetrate into its depth. This is a "light-giving obscurity" that teaches us "with a knowledge, without knowing, transcending all knowledge" (St. John of the Cross, *Spiritual Canticle*, n. 9, stanza 7).

This mystery of love is the mystery of the life of the Blessed Trinity, which is a life of communion and communication. As St. Ignatius tells us, love consists in sharing what one possesses and is (*Sp. Ex.* 231).

This exchange is something essential in the Trinity. The Father begets the Son communicating with him from all eternity the plenitude of his divine being; and the Son responds, also from all eternity, giving himself totally to the Father in an impulse of love (Jn. 1:1; 1 Jn. 1:1–3). The mystery of divine love is precisely in this, that the three persons, being infinitely perfect in themselves, communicate themselves fully giving their own being. This communication of love between the Father and the Son is so rich, so close and profound, and of such high quality (divine quality!) that it is also a person, the Holy Spirit. Each one of the three persons does not exist in itself and does not belong to itself, except in so far as it is referred and gives itself fully to the other two at the same time. The whole of their being is a pure and complete going out of themselves ("ecstasy"), a total tendency of each toward the others, in the expression of the Greek Fathers.

3. The Heart of Christ Reveals the Mystery of Man

In the light of the mystery of God we can more easily see in what man's perfection consists. Modern psychology has "rediscovered," in terms more comprehensible to modern man, what scholastic theology taught long ago. This teaching is that our human body (with its organs and senses) cannot grow and develop, or mature and reach its fullness except through a gradual process of acquisition. We consume food, assimilate concrete data, and acquire particular skills; but our person, our most recondite being, can only attain its plenitude and fulfilment by the opposite process. We develop ourselves, our persons, when we come out of our own selves as soon as we relate to others, and as far as we serve them. Jesus himself said, though this saying was not recorded in any of the Gospels: "There is more happiness in giving than in receiving" (Acts 20: 35). "God loves a cheerful giver" (2 Cor. 9:7).

The Heart of Christ is an open door that reveals to us, not only the interior life of the Trinity, but also God's exterior activity in the world. If love is always communicative of itself, the infinite love, which is God, wishes to communicate himself with all that is outside himself. Through creation he pours out his perfection to all created beings in the universe, making them all reflections of his infinite perfection.

In particular he has made man "to his image and likeness," capable of being, of communicating, of giving himself to others. In this sharing with others God has placed man's highest fulfilment of all his powers and his greatest happiness (Acts 20: 25).

Further God desires to make man a sharer in the communion of love and life which the essence of his trinitarian being (Jn. 17: 3, 21). This is precisely why the Son of God was sent to this world (Jn. 3: 16–17). Jesus Christ accomplishes this redeeming mission by his total self-giving, even to death on the cross. This was his voluntary offering of love and obedience to the Father and the surrender of his life for us, his brothers, thereby communicating to us his divine life, in the measure of which we are capable. "I came that they may have life, and have it abundantly" (Jn. 10: 10).

If we wish to go deeper into this knowledge of the love with which Jesus loves us, let us hear his words: "As the Father has loved me, so have I loved you" (Jn. 15:9). What can this mean? "As the Father has loved me." Jesus himself in the discourse of the last supper says: "That the love with which thou hast loved me may be in them (my disciples) and I in them" (Jn. 17: 36). It might look incredible that Jesus loved us with the same love with which he is loved by the Father. Yet, how could it be otherwise, once we share

16. Mystery of the Merciful Love

in the divine nature, as St. John tells us: "See what love the Father has given us, that we should be called children of God; and so we are" (1 Jn. 3: 1).

Following the same line of thought Jesus says: "This is my commandment, that you love one another as I have loved you" (Jn. 15: 12). Christian love, therefore, is to love with the only love that proceeds from the Father to the Son and "which has been poured into our hearts through the Holy Spirit which has been given to us." (Rom. 5: 5). Here is a perfect remedy for our egoism: we shall love with the same love which Christ communicates to us and which is a participation of that unique love of the Father to the Son.

4. History of Love and Mercy

His Holiness Pope John Paul II defines this revelation of love as mercy and says that "in man's history this revelation of love and mercy has taken a form and a name: that of Jesus Christ" (Encyclical *Redemptor Hominis*, 2, n. 9).

Hence derives the compassion towards all men, chiefly toward suffering humanity; hence the understanding of the position of others, with the desire of "being more ready to put a good interpretation on another's statement than to condemn it as false," as St. Ignatius would tell us (*Sp. Ex. 22*).

With this loving mercy "God our Savior desires all men to be saved and to come to the knowledge of the truth" (1 Tim. 2: 4). In other words, God wishes that all men become children of the Father. This imparts a profound meaning and an unshakable foundation to the apostolic labors in order that the word of God be accepted by all men; here lies the true motive of all evangelization.

The Pope himself has declared this in his encyclical letter: "Man cannot live without love. He would remain a being incomprehensible in himself; his life makes no sense, if love is not revealed to him, if he does not encounter love, if he does not experience it and make it his own, if he does not participate intimately in it. This is why Christ the Redeemer fully reveals man to himself" (Encyclical *Redemptor Hominis*, 2, n. 10).

It is clear from this that in order to understand man in his innermost being, that is to say, in order to penetrate into man's heart, that profound and original center of which we have spoken earlier, we must enter through the Heart of that Man-God, the God who made himself man in order that man be truly man and a child of God.

Only by entering through this door, which is the Heart of Christ, shall we be able to understand the greatness and holiness of God, our own dignity of being children of God in the deepest meaning of the human person, the foundation of the equality of all men before God, "in whom there is no partiality" (Eph. 6: 9), and who died for all, men and women, without distinction.

We shall thus understand also the eternal value and transcendence of our dedication to others in brotherly love, in which the perfection of the human person consists, and which impels us to collaborate in the Lord's plan of universal salvation, "as fellow workers with God" (l Cor. 3: 9).

Thus we shall feel that Jesus Christ, the Redeemer of man, while showing us his wounded Heart, tells us: "I am the door; if any one enters by me, he will be saved, and will go in and out and find pasture" (Jn. 10: 9).

17

FATHER ARRUPE'S SPIRITUAL TESTAMENT

Conclusion of His Address and Letter "Rooted and Grounded in Love"

Rome
February 6, 1981

Each year since 1978 the Ignatian Center of Spirituality, located in the Roman Curia of the Society of Jesus at Borgo S. Spirito, 5, Rome, has conducted a five-week program on Ignatian Spirituality. The lectures, given by well-known priests and professors from various countries, have been attended by a hundred or more seminarians, priests, and religious women and men. From 1978 to 1981, Father Arrupe gave the concluding lecture of the series. His four addresses have won widespread appreciation for their inspirational spirituality.

The last of these addresses was delivered on February 6, 1981, in the Hall of the General Congregations. Entitled with the Pauline expression "Rooted and Grounded in Love," it gives us the core of the speaker's Ignatian experience. He called it his own swan song, thinking probably of the resignation he intended to offer soon to a General Congregation.

The concluding section of it, brief and also the most intimate and personal, was pronounced with a special sincerity and emphasis which caused his hearers to listen in silence with attentive awe. This section turned out to be not only a resume of his discourses but also his spiritual testament. For later that year he suffered a stroke which left him largely incapacitated.

He later sent the discourse in the form of a letter to the whole Society.

Let me end now greeting you all, as well as every Jesuit who will read these pages, with that wonderful Pauline formula: *Peace be to the brethren, and love with faith, from God the Father and the Lord Jesus Christ. Grace be with all who love our Lord Jesus Christ with love undying.* [153]

The Center of the Ignatian Charism

Having reached this point, when we see that love is the very core of Christian—and therefore Ignatian—spirituality, I feel somewhat obliged to add a final consideration.

What I have said so far may be synthesized as follows:

1. Love (service) for our brothers, for Christ, for the Father, is the single and indivisible object of our charity.

2. Love resolves the dichotomies and tensions that can arise in an imperfectly understood Ignatian spirituality. For instance:

—*The tension between faith and justice* is resolved in charity. Faith has to be informed by charity, *'fides informata caritate,'* and so too must justice, which thus becomes a higher form of justice: it is charity that calls for justice.

—*The tension between one's own and one's neighbor's perfection.* Both should be the perfection of one and the same charity which tends to keep growing, as well intensively in itself, as extensively in the spread to and perfection of our fellow men.

—*The tension between prayer and active apostolic work* is resolved in the "contemplative in action," in seeking God in all things (the Contemplation for Attaining Love).

—*The tension among the three religious vows* disappears when their motivation and observance are inspired and impelled by charity (the same can be said of the fourth vow).

—*The tension between discernment and obedience.* Charity should be present both at the origin and in the final goal of discernment:

---

153. Eph. 6:23–24

the presence of this 'agape' enables us to discern God's will (Rom. 12:2), it is an intuition of charity (Eph. 3: 18–19; Col. 2: 2). Obedience similarly is an expression of that same divine will. Both superior and subject ought to be animated by charity, with the intuitiveness that is proper to love (Therrien: *Le discernment dans les écrits pauliniens*, p. 179).

3. Love is the solution to the apostolic problems created by the wickedness *(anomía)* of today's world.

4. Love is the very depth of the personality and work of Jesus Christ, that which gives unity to it all.

5. Love is also the deepest element of our life and activity, since with Jesus Christ we share one common Spirit (the Person, who is love), who makes us cry out like Christ: Abba, Father!

Love, then, understood in all its depth and breadth (both charity and mercy), is the synthesis of the whole life of Jesus Christ, and should be that of the Jesuit's whole life too.

Now, the natural symbol of love is the heart. The heart of Christ, therefore, is the natural symbol for representing and inspiring our personal and institutional spirituality, leading us to the very source and abyss of the human-divine love of Jesus Christ.

A Contradiction: Love and Silence?

And so, at the close of this address, I would like to tell the Society something that I believe I should not pass over in silence.

From my noviceship on, I have always been convinced that in the so-called "Devotion to the Sacred Heart" there is summed up a symbolic expression of the very core of the Ignatian spirit and an extraordinary power—*'ultra quam speraverint'*—both for personal perfection and for apostolic fruitfulness. This conviction is still mine today. It may have surprised some that during my generalate I have said relatively little on this topic. There was a reason for it, which we might call pastoral. In recent 'the Sacred Heart' has not failed to provoke emotional and allergic reactions in some, partly perhaps as a reaction to forms of presentation and terminology linked with tastes of a bygone age. So I thought it advisable to let some time go by, in the certainty that that attitude, more emotional than rational, would gradually change.

I cherished, and still do cherish, the conviction that the immense value of so deep a spirituality—which the Popes have termed excellent,[154] which employs so universal and so human a biblical symbol,[155] and a word, "heart," that is a genuine source—word (*Urwort*)—would before long come back in to usage.

For this reason, much to my regret, I have spoken and written relatively little on this subject, although I have often mentioned it in private conversation with individuals and find in this devotion one of the most profound affective sources of my interior life.

As I bring to an end this series of conferences on the Ignatian charism, I could not but give the Society an explanation for this silence of mine, which I trust will be understood. And at the same time, I did not wish to draw the pall of silence over my deep conviction that all of us, as the Society of Jesus, should reflect and discern before Christ crucified what this devotion has meant for the Society, and what it should mean even today. In today's circumstances, the world offers us challenges and opportunities that can be fully met only with the power of this love of the Heart of Christ.

A Last Message to the Society

This is the message that I wanted to communicate to you. There is no question of seeking to force or impose anything in an area where love precisely is involved. But I do wish to say: Give thought to this message, and *ponder on what presents itself to your mind.*[156] It would be sad if, having so great a treasure in our spirituality, even our institutional spirituality, we were to leave it aside for largely specious reasons.

If you want my advice, I would say to you, after 54 years of living in the Society and almost 16 of being its General, that there is a tremendous power latent in this devotion to the Heart of Christ. Each of us should discover it for himself—if he has not already

---

154. Cf Leo XIII, *Annum Sacrum*, 1899; Pius XI, *Miserentissi musRedemptor*, 1928; Pius XII *Haureitis Aquas*, 1956; Paul VI, *lnvestigabiles Divitias*, 1965.
155. Eph. I:18.

17. His Spiritual Testament

done so—and then, entering deeply into it, apply it to his personal life in whatever way the Lord may suggest and grant. There is here an extraordinary grace that God offers us.

The Society needs the *"dynamis"* contained in this symbol and in the reality that it proclaims: the love of the Heart of Christ. Perhaps what we need is an act of ecclesial humility, to accept what the Supreme Pontiffs, the General Congregations and the Generals of the Society have incessantly repeated. And yet, I am convinced that there could be few proofs of the spiritual renewal of the Society so clear as a widespread and vigorous devotion to the Heart of Jesus. Our apostolate would receive new strength and we would see its effects very soon, both in our personal lives and in our apostolic activities.

Let us not fall into the presumptuous temptation of considering ourselves superior to a devotion that is expressed in a symbol or in a graphic representation of it. Let us not join *the wise and prudent of this world* from whom the Father keeps hidden his truths and mysteries, while he reveals them to those who are or make themselves *little ones*.[157] Let us have that simplicity of heart which is the first condition for a profound conversion: *Unless you change and make yourselves like little children.*[158] Those are Christ's words, and we might translate them in this way: "If you want, as individuals and as a Society, to enter into the treasures of the Kingdom and to help build it up with an extraordinary effectiveness, make yourselves like the poor whom you wish to serve. You keep on saying so often that the poor have taught you more than many books; learn from them, thrn, this very simple lesson: acknowledge my love in my Heart."

---

156. Sp. Ex. 53.
157. Lk. 11:21; Mt. 11:25.
158. Mt. 18:3.

REFLECTIONS IN RETROSPECT

By Ignacio Iglesias S.J.
Former Provincial of Spain
Till 1981 Regional Assistant for Spain in Rome

Christ comes alive in the writings and the life of Fr. Arrupe. This is demonstrated by the preceding selection of texts and by many others, all in fact. They may not deal directly with Christ but cannot be understood without him, a Christ who is most personally lived and "interiorly felt."

When he celebrated his Golden Jubilee as a Jesuit (1977), I was requested to write something and made an attempt to sketch the peculiar Christ of Fr. Arrupe. I think the statements made at that time are as valid today and even confirmed as the conclusion of this book.

The Christ of Fr. Arrupe

Sometimes I have heard Jesuits discuss Fr. Arrupe's Christology. Is it classic or modern and up-to-date? I think this is a useless discussion and, I would even say, banal. I can certainly bear witness to the fact that I have seen on his table (and I confess my curiosity) the books of the new Christologists of various tendencies, from the masters of the North Schillebeeckx, Soonenberg, Galot... to the latest of the Latin American Christology, González Faus and Jon Sobrino.

But this is beside the point. What really matters to the Society is not his Christology but his Christ. The Christ he lives, proclaims and communicates as "seen and heard" by him. What matters is his personal knowledge, his personal experience of Christ. (I am aware of the many reservations that Psychology and Sociology show concerning the "experiences" of God lived and reported by man.) Nevertheless, in the real life of so many men, from Paul of Tarsus up to Mother Theresa of Calcutta, these experiences are so profoundly real that they must deeply affect and influence life, even granting that they are mysterious and beyond grasp in themselves.

So we are concerned with the particular form in which Fr. Arrupe has been "touched" and "reached" (Phil. 3:12) by Christ. This is certainly something difficult to express, but it brings about effects and attitudes affecting everyday life, like the *"sensus Christi"* so often mentioned by him in his conversations, and the lack of which pains him more than other defects of ours.

I beg your indulgence if I dare describe very briefly this Christ of Fr. Arrupe.

He is, first of all and basically, the Christ of St. Ignatius of Loyola, with some distinctive nuances. He is to be found everywhere in his writings. I take the liberty of summing up the salient features, those more frequently stressed:

—He is a trinitarian Christ, with whom we can "be sent" and through whom we gain access to the Father: "What type of encounter, dialogue, or union, or docility to the spirit of Christ, are we trying to bring into our lives? Behind the words (always approximations), we must find once again the simple truth, and draw forth its consequences: Christ lives, speaks, acts by receiving from the Father his being, his word, his action. And so it is with us, *"in Christo."* By participating in his relations with his Father our whole existence unfolds" (ARSI XV (1971), 736).

—He is the Christ of the Incarnation and the meditation of the Kingdom, Son and Sent in one indivisible personal reality, who takes upon himself a suffering mankind and creates a new man and a new world: "The young will be helped to meet God ... if they learn to look at the manifold misery of men that clamors for a Savior. The apostle will always come up against human misery. How much will the Jesuit gain in humble generosity and apostolic magnanimity if he puts on Christ, accepting himself and the others" (ARSI XV (1967), 115).

—He is the Christ of *kenosis* and of Easter who has to be followed with personal love "till the end" (Jn. 13:1) in the third degree of humility, the only way to really become "conformed to the image of the Son ... the first-born of many brothers" (Rom. 8:29). This image of Christ, "a man for others" inspired all the interventions of Fr. Arrupe at the International Congress of Jesuit Alumni in Valencia (1974), which impressed listeners and readers very profoundly and in a very wide circle: "We must emphasize that the radical novelty of the Gospel consists in proclaiming this peculiar humanism, this new model of man, risen from faith in Jesus: man dead to all forms of selfishness, and by rising again, 'born from above,' free to love in truth, free to give his own life, free to fully commit himself to the service of others... The man finally who, integrating in the intimate unity of himself as a person faith and love, love of God and love of neighbor, makes real and visible all the social implications of our faith in Jesus and thus becomes like Jesus himself 'a man for others'" (July 1, 1978).

—He is the Christ of personal friendship, of the confident dialogue (see the text of the various prayers composed by Fr. Arrupe), of hope ("Christ Jesus our hope," 1 Tim. 1:1): "The young must be encouraged to maintain continually a fraternal and real dialogue with the living Christ, present in the sufferings and aspirations of men in the crisis of the time and the progress of the Church; with Christ, who calls us personally to share with him the cross and the glory of saving the world" (ARSI XV (1967), 115).

—He is the Christ who lives and works in the Church especially through his Vicar: In the concluding homily of GC 32, during the concelebration held at St. Peter's Basilica (March 6, 1975), after highlighting the "ecclesial transformation" that led Ignatius of Loyola to his special "devotion" to the Vicar of Christ, he concludes as follows: "From that moment on, the new criterion to 'save souls' will be for Ignatius the recourse to the Vicar of Christ; 'he was convinced,' says Nadal, 'that Christ would deign to guide him in the life of divine service through his Vicar' (MN I, 264). In Ignatius' mystical experience, the Roman Pontiff will appear increasingly as the Vicar of Christ, and the full and concrete consecration of Ignatius and his companions to the Eternal King will be in future a total availability to the Vicar of Christ on earth ... "

—He is the Christ of the Eucharist, whom he has thus addressed publicly not long ago: "For me intimate conversation with you, really present in the Eucharist and waiting for me in the tabernacle, has always been and still is a source of inspiration and strength: without them I would not be able to carry on, much less bear the burden of my responsibilities. The Holy Sacrifice of the Mass is the center of my life. I cannot imagine a single day without celebrating or taking part in the sacrificial meal of the Eucharist. Without Mass my life would be empty, I would lack the strength: I feel this deeply and state so".

The Vision of La Storta

It is impossible to conclude this brief sketch without referring to another personal experience. Rereading Fr. Arrupe's writings, I seem to have understood—a little at least—the intimate reason why he so often mentions the vision of La Storta. It is simply because this figure of Christ sums up the Christ he has lived. It is with this Christ that he tries to link his whole personal experience in the following of Jesus, which he wanted to be the experience of each and every one of us in the Society. On the occasion of the renewal of the Society's consecration to the Sacred Heart of Jesus (June 9, 1972) he placed himself and wanted to place the whole Society in that little chapel of La Storta and in the heart of that experience, the sum and synthesis of so many other experiences of Ignatius. And here is the trinitarian Christ, Son and Sent, here the union of God and the mission, here the *kenosis* of the standard of the Cross, here the realism of the following of Christ to Rome under his Vicar, here the Christ of hope, of Easter, of work... "If anyone wants to follow me..."

This figure of a Christ mysteriously unified in his intimate being as God and man, in which his mission and the will of the Father is lived as such, the will of the Father becoming a mission, attracts Ignatius of Loyola forcefully and constitutes the unifying center of the "contemplative in action" according to Nadal's definition.

This figure, according to his own words, continues to attract Fr. Arrupe. The concern for this synthesis in the following of Christ so that union with God and mission may form an indestructible unity is the fundamental theme of his letter of November 1, 1981 to the whole Society and is easily identifiable in all his writings.

"Let us maintain the principle: to open oneself outwards, one has to open himself no less inwards, that is towards Christ. The one who has to reach out to help human needs must dialogue more intensely with Christ. If one must become a contemplative in action, he has to find in the intensity of his every action the urgency to a deeper contemplation. If we want to be open to the world, we must do so as Christ did, so that our witness springs, as his did, from his life and his doctrine. Let us not shrink from becoming, like him. a sign of contradiction and a stumbling block ... For the rest, not even he was understood by many."

This is what I wrote in 1977. Now I confirm it. This Christ is all love of the Father and that is why, forgetful of self, he is all *for* man. Rather, more properly and biblically, he is all *for the sake of* all men. For him every man is not only a recipient of love but a 'motive' profoundly assimilated.

This assimilation of man in the depths of God is nothing else than the saying that "God so loved the world that. . ." It has its full theological and real 'locus' in the Heart of Christ, where the person appropriates those for whom he is, lives, works and dies. It is also where every human being who lets himself be appropriated by Christ can discover his personal 'reason' to exist and to act, the center in which he can recreate himself according to God's original plan as a man (or a woman) *for* Christ and *for* every brother...

Pedro Arrupe has made his life a voyage into this 'locus.' He has increasingly centered his life in it, simplifying it, and has built up his work on it. The preceding text reveals this secret of his.

Like John the Apostle, who had no other word to say in his old age but "Love one another," this veteran fighter and apostle, reduced to physical helplessness today, has wanted to collect and sum up his 'reason' in these pages and take us to the center of the Gospel with his personal style. We close them with reverence and with the conviction that we have entered (or at least peeped, thanks to him) into the innermost sanctuary of God, from which Christ reconstructs everything, fills everything, gives everything, is everything: his **HEART.**

Ignacio Iglesias S.J.
Madrid, September 9, 1983

FATHER ARRUPE'S FAREWELL HOMILY AT LA STORTA

Rome: September 4, 1983

*One day after his resignation
and before the election of a new General*

On September 3, 1983, with express sentiments of deepest regret and of profoundest gratitude to Father Arrupe for his extraordinary services in his eighteen years as the General of the Society of Jesus, the members of the 33rd General Congregation voted to accept the resignation of the Society's esteemed leader.

In the evening session of the same day Father Arrupe came into the hall. The text of his message was read to the Congregation members and to the other Jesuit representatives of the Roman communities. Father Paolo Dezza, the Papal Delegate, stated that it was a difficult task to express adequately the gratitude all Jesuits felt for Father Arrupe's services during so many years. He recalled that requests had come in to the General Congregation from many provinces asking for this act of collective gratitude.

The following day, Sunday. September 4, the entire group of Congregation members and other Jesuits from Rome gathered in the evening in the basilica next to the to the recently restored chapel of La Storta for the concelebration of a Eucharistic liturgy with Father Pedro Arrupe. During the Mass a homily prepared by Father Arrupe was read for him by one of the Assistants.

This occasion was remarkable in several ways. It framed the outpouring from the heart of a revered father and leader who, when reduced to silence and inactivity, expressed in his own way his gratitude to God and to the Society.

The former General felt that like veteran Simeon of the Temple of Jerusalem and pilgrim Ignatius at the wayside shrine of La Storta on his arrival in Rome, he had been

> *granted his ardent desire of seeing the Savior of the world and of being placed by God the Father with Christ his Son. He had certainly shared the experience of carrying his cross. If the day's celebration was for him a farewell and a conclusion, he hoped it would also be the beginning of a new period of service with fresh enthusiasm.*
>
> *The twenty-eighth General of the Society, in union with the Founder and first General, "felt himself drawn to the Heart of Christ" in that visit to La Storta, where the Company received the call to service and the assurance of divine assistance.*
>
> *For Father Arrupe, the word 'heart,' taken in the biblical sense, comes close to a definition of the whole person of Christ—his intellect, his will, his emotional life, in brief, all that we mean by the word 'personality.' Hence it was natural for him to write in his earlier study (page 75 above) that we "refer to the Heart of Christ in order to sum up in one word all the values which we find in his person. There is no other expression more apt to convey 'the breadth and the length, the height and the depth (of) the love of Christ, which is beyond all knowledge' (Eph. 3: 18)."*
>
> *We can well say that this final message at La Storta constituted for Father Arrupe his personal Legacy of the Heart to the whole Society.*

*

It is in many ways fitting that at the conclusion of my ministry as Superior General of the Society of Jesus, I should come here to La Storta to sing my *"Nunc Dimittis"*—even though it be in the silence imposed by my present condition.

The veteran Simeon, at the close of a long life of service, and in the magnificent splendor of the Temple of Jerusalem, attained his ardent desire when he received the child Jesus in his arms and drew him to his heart. In the very modest chapel of La Storta, Ignatius of Loyola, when about to begin a new life of service as Founder and first General of our Society, felt himself drawn to the Heart of Christ: "God the Father placed him with Christ his Son," according to his own earnest prayer to the Virgin Mary.

I would not dare compare myself to these two outstanding servants of the Lord. But I can affirm that I have always had a great devotion to the experience of Ignatius at La Storta, and that I am immensely consoled at finding myself in this hallowed place to give thanks to God on arriving at journey's end. "For my eyes have seen your salvation." How often in these eighteen years I have had proof of God's faithfulness to his promise: "I will be favorable to you in Rome."

A profound experience of the loving protection of divine providence has been my strength in bearing the burden of my responsibilities and facing the challenges of our day. True, I have had my difficulties, both big and small; but never has God failed to stand by me. And now more than ever I find myself in the hands of this God who has taken hold of me.

The liturgy of this Sunday seems just made to express my sentiments on this occasion. Like St. Paul I can say that I am "an old man, and now also a prisoner of Christ Jesus." I had planned things differently; but it is God who disposes, and his designs are a mystery: "Who can divine the will of the Lord?" But we do know the will of the Father, that we become true images of the Son; and the Son tells us clearly in the Gospel: "Anyone who does not carry his cross and come after me cannot be my disciple."

Father Laínez, from whom we have the words of the promise, "I will be favorable," proceeds to explain that Ignatius never understood them to mean that he and his companions would be free of suffering. On the contrary: he was convinced that they were called to serve Christ carrying his cross, "he felt he saw Christ, with the cross on his back, and the eternal Father by his side, saying to him: 'I want that you take this man as your servant.' And so Jesus took him, saying: 'I want that you serve us.' Because of this, conceiving great devotion to this Most Holy Name, he wished to call our fellowship: 'the Society of Jesus.'"

This name had already been chosen by the companions before they came to Rome to offer their services to the Pope. But it received a very special confirmation from the experience at La Storta. One can notice a close relationship between the phrases employed by Laínez and those of the Formula of the Institute approved by Julius

III: "Whoever wishes to enlist under the standard of the Cross as a soldier of God in our Society, which we desire to be distinguished by the name of Jesus, and to serve the Lord alone and the Church his Bride, under the Roman Pontiff, the Vicar of Christ on earth..."

What was for Ignatius the culmination and summing up of so many special graces received since his conversion, was for the Society a pledge that it would share in the graces of the Founder in the measure in which it remained faithful to the inspiration that gave it birth. I pray that this celebration, that is for me a farewell and a conclusion, be for you and for the whole Society represented here, the beginning of a new period of service, with fresh enthusiasm. May the collaboration of the whole Society in the renovation of the chapel of La Storta be an abiding symbol and an unfailing inspiration for a united effort at spiritual renewal, trusting in the graces whose memory is enshrined in La Storta. I shall remain at your side with my prayers.

Like St. Ignatius, I implore the Virgin Mary that we may all be placed with her Son; and that as Queen and Mother of the Society she be with you in all the labors of the General Congregation, and especially in the election of the new General.

ANOTHER MESSAGE TO A PROVINCIAL

In the course of the General Congregation, the Provincial of the Wisconsin Province of the United States, Fr. Joseph Labaj, had to leave Rome because of illness—cancer of the throat which it was feared would be terminal. Before his departure, the ailing provincial received a farewell message from the ailing Father Arrupe. Here is how Father Labaj communicated the final exhortation to his men in a letter dated October 13, 1983:

At the General Congregation, my room was in the infirmary, right next to Father Arrupe's. So I was able to pop in on him every day a couple of times and just smile my cheery smile and say hello. When I told him I was leaving, I asked his blessing which he gave me and also said he blesses the Province, too, but he gave me a special reference to what he had written at the end of his talk, "Rooted and Grounded in Love," on devotion to the Sacred Heart, and I would like to close with this particular thought. He said, "Here are Christ's words for us: 'If you want to enter into the treasures of the Kingdom and to help build it up with extraordinary effectiveness, make yourselves more like the poor whom you wish to serve. Learn from them then the very simple lesson: Acknowledge my love in my Sacred Heart.'"

Sincerely in the Sacred Heart,
(sd) Joseph J. Labaj, S.J.